A VERY SHORT,
FAIRLY INTERESTING AND
REASONABLY CHEAP BOOK ABOUT
COACHING AND MENTORING

Also in this series:

Chris Grey, *A Very Short, Fairly Interesting and Reasonably Cheap Book about Studying Organizations*, 2nd edition

Brad Jackson and Ken Parry, *A Very Short, Fairly Interesting and Reasonably Cheap Book about Studying Leadership*, 2nd edition

Chris Carter, Stewart Clegg and Martin Kornberger, *A Very Short, Fairly Interesting and Reasonably Cheap Book about Studying Strategy*

Ann L. Cunliffe, *A Very Short, Fairly Interesting and Reasonably Cheap Book about Management*

George Cairns and Martyna Sliwa, *A Very Short, Fairly Interesting and Reasonably Cheap Book about International Business*

Jim Blythe, *A Very Short, Fairly Interesting and Reasonably Cheap Book about Studying Marketing*

Irena Grugulis, *A Very Short, Fairly Interesting and Reasonably Cheap Book about Studying Human Resource Management*

A VERY SHORT, FAIRLY INTERESTING AND REASONABLY CHEAP BOOK ABOUT COACHING AND MENTORING

BOB GARVEY

Los Angeles | London | New Delhi
Singapore | Washington DC

First published 2011

This title for the 'Very Short, Fairly Interesting and Reasonably Cheap Book about...Series' was devised by Chris Grey. His book, *A Very Short, Fairly Interesting and Reasonably Cheap Book about Studying Organizations*, was the founding title of this series.

Chris Grey asserts his rights to be recognized as founding editor of the **Very Short, Fairly Interesting and Reasonably Cheap Book about...Series**

SAGE Publications Ltd
1 Oliver's Yard
55 City Road
London EC1Y 1SP

SAGE Publications Inc.
2455 Teller Road
Thousand Oaks, California 91320

SAGE Publications India Pvt Ltd
B 1/I 1 Mohan Cooperative Industrial Area
Mathura Road
New Delhi 110 044

SAGE Publications Asia-Pacific Pte Ltd
33 Pekin Street #02-01
Far East Square
Singapore 048763

Library of Congress Control Number: 2011923060

British Library Cataloguing in Publication data

A catalogue record for this book is available from the British Library

ISBN 978-1-84920-782-9
ISBN 978-1-84920-783-6 (pbk)

Typeset by C&M Digitals (P) Ltd, Chennai, India
Printed in India at Replika Press Pvt Ltd
Printed on paper from sustainable resources

Dedication

To Margaret for always supporting, challenging, questioning and being so creative. Thank you!

Contents

About the Author

Bob Garvey is one of Europe's leading academic practitioners in coaching and mentoring and his research has influenced policy, practice and productivity in a range of organisations in all sectors – corporate, small business, public and the not for profit and voluntary sectors. He is also in demand internationally as a keynote conference speaker and has presented papers and keynote conference presentations around the world including the US, Canada, Europe and Africa. He was awarded a Chair in Mentoring and Coaching at Sheffield Hallam University in 2007. Bob is widely published in books as well as professional and academic journals. His current clients include Lloyds Banking Group, Wood McKenzie, McBride plc, SIG, Earth Tech, SSAT, Eli Lilly, several universities in Europe and a variety of NHS Trusts. Bob has coaching experience with executives in a range of sectors, self-employed people, young people, performing artists and middle management.

Introduction: Why Developing a Critical Perspective on Coaching and Mentoring Matters

This book is about raising questions and offering a range of research and practice-based arguments to stimulate and provoke debate. If you feel stimulated, inspired, provoked, irritated or cross, then this book is doing its job! If you get an emotional reaction of any kind, pay attention to it and critically reflect on it. If you are indifferent, I have failed!

I am an academic practitioner. The practitioner element of my work is about continually trying to develop my practice and gain experience. The academic part recognises that this happens through developing critical reflection and critical reflexivity about these experiences. This means that I both practise coaching and mentoring (C&M) activity and I research them, read about them, discuss them with others – in fact, I am a little bit obsessed! Perhaps I need some C&M!

Some years ago a colleague of mine with whom I had done considerable academic practitioner work on mentoring said *'I think we have done mentoring'*. I was shocked because in my view it will never be possible to have 'done mentoring' anymore that it would be possible to have 'done coaching'. This is because mentoring, as an educational process, has a very long history that is directly traceable to the Ancient Greeks. It has undergone many changes in approach and philosophy. It is socially embedded and dynamic. It has been subject to fads and, at times, has become a social epidemic and a central plank of government policies on both sides of the Atlantic. This is also because coaching as a developmental process is a relative newcomer, although many people would make associative links to Ancient history. It has also undergone huge dynamic changes in approach and philosophy and has now started to become a serious player in commercial life as well as a substantial business in its own right. In social matters (and coaching and mentoring are social matters), experience is important and rooted in history. The brilliance of history is that it repeats itself repeatedly but the challenge is to learn something from it so as not to repeat the same mistakes repeatedly! This book is about thinking new thoughts!

For both coaching and mentoring, it is the rapid adoption and dynamic metamorphosis through social application that is interesting and this means that there is always going to be change. The enthusiasm with which mentoring and coaching are embraced is interesting and the debates which surround them are interesting. The fact that the various forms of coaching and mentoring activities are located within capitalist economies is also interesting.

For me, this all means that it is never possible to have 'done either' because there is always something new to learn. If the day ever comes when that is no longer the case, I will have 'done' mentoring and coaching but somehow I do not think that will ever happen!

So, let us reflect on some data. Coaching and mentoring (C&M) activities are fast growing and developing across the world. In the UK, C&M are widespread throughout all types of organisation – public, private, large, small and not-for-profit. For example, in recent years, the UK Home Office has spent £10million per annum on mentoring for young offenders; the DfES has spent £25million on young people's schemes, and in the NHS approximately 250,000 people are engaged in a mentoring activity (or 20 per cent of all staff). In the field of executive coaching, expenditure in both the private and public sectors is still high at approximately £200 per hour per executive. Coaching and mentoring activities are in other sectors as well including the voluntary sector, SMEs and Education.

The Bresser Global Survey of Coaching (2008/9) and the Bresser European Survey of Coaching both showed that there were estimated 43,000–45000 business coaches currently operating worldwide. There is a wide distribution across the world but the greatest intensity of coaching activity can be found in 20 per cent of the world's population in Europe, North America and Australia where it is estimated that 80 per cent of all business coaches of the world practise. With nearly 30 per cent of the EU population, the UK and Germany accommodate over 70 per cent of all EU coaches (UK – 7500; Germany – 5000). The UK and Ireland have the highest density of operating coaches (about one business coach per 8000 inhabitants). According to this survey, there is no doubt that coaching activity is on the rise within the whole of Europe and across the globe.

Throughout the coaching and mentoring industry, there is concern about standards, competencies and codes of ethics. Here, C&M practitioners are looking to bodies like the European Mentoring and Coaching Council (EMCC) and the International Coaching Federation (ICF) to establish guidelines for best practice and universities in Europe and the USA are increasingly beginning to develop accredited programmes to address the standards issue. Added to this, private sector consultancies are flooding the market with a range of training offers, particularly for coaching.

Psychologists and therapists are getting in on the act as well. There is an ongoing debate in the coaching literature (Brunning, 2006; Hart et al., 2007; Kilburg, 2004) on the role of psychology in executive coaching in particular. This generally focuses on the distinction between psychotherapy and coaching, which is a similar debate to that found in coaching and mentoring. Additionally, Grant and O'Hara (2006) speculate that '*some individuals seek coaching as a socially-acceptable form of therapy*'. In support of Grant and O'Hara but with a sting in the tail, Williams and Irving (2001: 3–7) state '*Coaching looks like counselling in disguise – without the stigma, but also without the ethics*'. To add to the ethical debate, in an article by Bono et al. (2009) the authors observe that qualified psychologists charge more for coaching than they do for therapy and more than non-psychologist coaches for their services and that they derive 50 per cent of their income from coaching. This suggests that there is a commercial interest here. These points are discussed later.

Overall, coaching, in particular, is a major growth industry and mentoring activity is extensive and stable. Both remain unregulated; however, regulation is, as is argued later in the book, a problematic issue and in some ways just as problematic as non-regulation.

Then there is the issue of research. Mentoring has a long record of a particular approach to research (Garvey et al., 2009), especially in the USA, but for coaching there is little to be found other than output studies, Return on Investment (ROI) studies, and accounts that are mainly written by coaches themselves or coaching consultancies along with a number of practitioner-based studies. Lowman (2005: 90) states that executive coaching has '*caught on more as an area of practice than as one of theory or research*'. This situation is showing signs of change as more research is beginning to appear.

Also, there is much conflicting literature on what coaching and mentoring are and often those who write about coaching will make negative comments about mentoring and those who write about mentoring will make negative comments about coaching (Clutterbuck & Megginson, 2005: 15–17).

In addition to all this there is the issue of commercialisation. Coaching in particular is present across society and growing. The dominant arena at present is visible in coaching consultancy where large sums of money can be made. I do not have a problem with this but I do have a problem with those individuals and organisations that become very vocal about ethics, standards and professionalisation while also being highly concerned about the maximisation of their own profits – a clear case of double standards and inappropriate reflection en masse!

I was at a conference last year where one participant declared publicly that maximising his business was his sole reason for attending the event. The comment made me bristle a bit because I was under the rather naive impression that conferences were about continuous professional development, the exchange of ideas, practice and research, and developing critical thought. However, he was at least being open and honest about his intent and this gave people the opportunity to make an informed choice about whether or not to engage with him. An example of critical thought in action!

On the other hand, I bought a book the other day and was struck by the title *Where Were the Coaches When the Banks Went Down?* (Blakey and Day 2009). I also thought this would be an interesting discussion of coaches' roles and responsibilities during the credit crunch. I also thought it would raise issues of practice and ethics and discuss collusion and relationship power dynamics. It did not. What it did do was mention these things in passing and then get on with promoting an alternative coaching process model that was based, it stated, on the learning from the banking crisis. A good solution-oriented coaching idea I think. However, there were also implications from this that this new model could have helped us avoid the crisis or at least could stop it happening again. For me, this seemed to miss the point.

On the plus side, the model presented was interesting, well constructed and made practical and ethical sense. As a concept, this practical model promised to address important issues in executive coaching. In some ways, it uncritically does so.

On the minus side, there is only anecdotal and impressionistic evidence to support the claims made, while issues of power, responsibility, fees and relationship are not tackled critically. It is yet another un-critical practitioner book written by practitioners who are promoting their own business. It is interesting to observe that these authors cite Darwinism as a starting point for their discussion. This 'linking' or associative technique is a common device that is used by coaching writers in particular. Does this approach provide credibility? I will discuss this point later.

I have also learnt that there is a series of seminars with the same title travelling around the UK under the auspices of the Association of Coaching. The marketing machine for these is in full swing! So, on one level, good on those folks for having an idea and promoting and developing it, that is what we have come to expect in this unregulated world. But on another – how honest is this title in the current climate? And whose interests are being served here? I am sure there are many. We can all recognise the amoral capitalist game, even if it is not made explicit, and we can still be caught by it!

In my case it was the title and the endorsements made by the very eminent coaching people who were joining in with the discourse that drew me to buy the book. Maybe I should have been less naive or less grumpy but I do wonder about how many others made the same assumptions as me. Certainly, one of my students sent me an invitation to a seminar on the book with a disparaging comment attached, so there is at least one other! I did consider going to see what it was all about but I would have resented having to pay £40 to do so when I had just read the book! I was left feeling uncomfortable and somewhat irritated and that is not a good outcome. Maybe it's the world we now live in today where everyone is after a piece of the action: everyone can be famous for that fifteen minutes as we become more and more individualistic and less socially minded.

In thinking about this issue, I recollected a powerful and challenging quote by Will Hutton (1997: 4)

> One lesson of our time may be that capitalism has triumphed for the moment in the great battle with socialism … But the moral and religious values which informed the socialist and social democratic movements of the twentieth century, along with their fierce advocacy of liberty, cannot be consigned to history without endangering the civilisation which we prize … the operation of the unchecked market has an inherent tendency to produce unreasonable inequality, economic instability and immense concentrations of private, unaccountable power. To protect itself, society has to have countervailing powers built into the operation of the market, otherwise it cannot deliver its promise. Instead it collapses into licence masquerading as liberty, spivvery dressed up as risk-taking and exploitation in the guise of efficiency and flexibility.

The significance of this prophecy, made in 1997, is very striking in the context of the banking crisis some ten years later! The philosopher Bertrand Russell once commented *'Advocates of capitalism are very apt to appeal to the sacred principles of liberty, which are embodied in one maxim: The fortunate must not be restrained in the exercise of tyranny over the unfortunate'* (Russell, 1928). With a central discourse in both coaching and mentoring of liberty, perhaps there are resonances here for the context in which these activities happen?

And then there is the issue of camps. Gibb and Hill (2006) and Clutterbuck and Megginson (2005: 15–17) suggest that we are witnessing a polarisation of different branches of coaching and mentoring that is becoming almost tribal in nature. These 'tribes' often draw strength from the knowledge base from which they draw their narrative. For example, Stelter (2009) suggests that many business leaders are attracted to ideas within the sports world and that they adopt these to develop the competitiveness, motivation and performance of their employees. This aspect is discussed in Chapters 1 and 5.

and the point ... ?

The consequence of the above gives rise to a dominant discourse that coaching and mentoring *'are good'* – *except* if you are a coach commenting on mentoring or a mentor commenting on coaching!

Let me put my cards on the table. I am *'for'* coaching and mentoring. I participate as a coach and coachee, mentor and mentee, and I write about them, read about them, research them, give presentations about them, and teach others about them. Obviously I am biased as well! However, I am also an academic and I consider my role in society is to provide a critique of the things I study in order to inform understanding and to help others make informed choices. Offering such a critique comes with risks attached. I know that some people find such a challenge difficult and will take it personally. At best, readers may value the alternative perspectives I present. In the middle, I could (hopefully) be viewed as a likeable if grumpy old academic who must be tolerated but who doesn't know much about the 'real' world. At worst what I write could be viewed as offensive, insulting, ignorant, arrogant, or rude. In my work on coaching and mentoring I have been accused of all the above.

One prominent academic was so offended by what we had said about their work that we engaged in an email exchange that lasted several months. I tried very hard to discuss the issues raised by this colleague and I studied what we had written all over again but could see nothing other than a normal critical academic debate. I sent this colleague a copy of the book and invited them to read all of it before we had further discussions. They declined and only focused on the offending section. Ultimately, I commented that we could agree to disagree. I received no reply.

Business people have also accused me of not being in the *'real'* world. I still wonder where this *'real'* world is and what world I am actually in right now sitting on a train travelling to Manchester! I do not think that 'reality' is a simple figure of speech. It means something far more important and fundamental than that.

A few years ago, I was presenting a paper on the benefits of mentoring across all sectors to a mixed audience. One of the participants, who had come in late, offered me a challenge. He said *'You academics make me sick, where's the measurement, where's the proof and never a straight answer?'* I replied, *'And people like you make me sick because you think everything can be reduced to cause and effect. Do you think mentoring is like that motorcar in the car park outside? A mechanical devise which you fix with a spanner?' Or is it a living and dynamic relationship?'* The pro-mentoring audience gave me a loud round of applause.

This person was financing the research but that fact did not, in my view, bring with it special rights of rudeness for either of us! Nor did it mean that I should have done anything other than what I did do. Of course he had a point, but so did I. In my view, such rational pragmatic thinking as was displayed by this manager dominates the business world. How far has this thinking been helpful and constructive and how far has it been destructive and unhelpful for human progress?

If that sounds like an essay question then it probably has been, but it does not mean that these questions are worthless or that human activities such as coaching and mentoring can be reduced to cause and effect. If it were that simple, we would have all the world's human problems solved by now!

As this book unfolds I will discuss the idea of 'reality' particularly within mentoring and coaching activities and invite you, the reader, to consider the discourse you subscribe to and what its implications might be for your practice.

As I said at the start of this Introduction, if the words in this book create feelings within you then that is a good thing, reflect on them, explore them, question what has created the reaction, and seek evidence to help with your thinking. Indeed try to coach or mentor yourself and seek out some alternatives – just because you think something this does not make it the truth!

So, to quote from that brilliant children's book *Where the Wild Things Are* by Maurice Sendak (1963), *Let the wild rumpus begin!*

1

What is Mentoring and What is Coaching?

This chapter covers the historical narratives of coaching and mentoring and links these to modern day practice and current arguments. It also explores the historical meanings and considers what coaching and mentoring are for. It is clear that there have been changes in meaning for the terms 'coaching' and 'mentoring' over time. This observation in turn raises 'truth' issues. I discuss these by making use of a speculative unified heuristic framework for coaching and mentoring at the end of the chapter.

introduction

Before I get into presenting a brief history of coaching and mentoring, I think it is important to be mindful of what historical research could become. Friedrich Nietzsche's essay, *The Use and Abuse of History* (1873), talked about a *'malignant historical fever'*. Nietzsche believed that studying history was potentially a worthless activity, which did not always lead to a good use for historical tradition. He believed that past knowledge should serve both the present and the future but also that history should not become abstract and devoid of the context that gave it life. Social context is a recurrent theme throughout this book!

A concept to consider, and one that underpins this book, is that both coaching and mentoring share a learning and development agenda (see Chapter 5). There are many ways to look at learning. For example:

- The importance of whole person learning (Buber, 1958).
- The conditions for learning, the social context and dialogue (Rogers, 1969; Habermas, 1974; Vygotsky, 1978, 1981, 1985a, b; and Bruner, 1990).
- The importance of experiential learning (Dewey, 1958; Lewin, 1951; Piaget, 1970 and Kolb, 1984).
- The importance of reflection (Argyris & Schon, 1981).
- The importance of purpose (Lyotard, 1984).

In relation to this 'purpose' for coaching and mentoring activity, Lyotard's (1984) framework as summarised by Pedler et al. (2005: 62) is helpful here:

> Speculative: knowledge for its own sake, concerned with theoretical rigour, unconcerned with application.
>
> Emancipatory: knowledge that helps us overcome oppression and attain the highest human potential.
>
> Performative: knowledge that helps action in the world, to resolve problems, to produce better goods and services.

Lyotard's position suggests that learning has the potential to serve all three purposes. However, arguably, modern life seems to focus far more on performative knowledge and this, in my view, creates a problem, placing all sorts of tensions and pressures on people. It also raises ethical issues and we could well ask – *'if the purpose of coaching and or mentoring varies or is mixed, does the practice and therefore the "in use" meaning change?'*

These issues are discussed as the book develops.

a very brief history of mentoring

The first mention of mentoring in history can be found in Homer's Odyssey. Here Mentor, the Goddess Athene in disguise, takes Odysseus' son on a developmental journey in order to maintain the Kingdom of Ithaca and develop a successor to the throne.

Much later on in eighteenth-century Europe there appeared five main publications about mentoring. First was Fénélon's (1651–1715) educational treaties *Les Aventures de Télémaque*; then Louis Antonine de Caraccioli (1723–1803) published *Veritable le Mentor ou l'education de la noblesse* in 1759 and this was translated into English in 1760 to become *The true mentor, or, an essay on the education of young people in fashion*. In 1793 and 1796, Honoria published three volumes of *The Female Mentor*. The later authors all based their writing on Fénélon.

These historical works link mentoring with cognitive development, emotional development, leadership and social integration, all of these being rooted in an experiential learning philosophy. Mentors invited mentees to participate in and observe situations that they would then discuss. Transition and change are also key elements and mentoring will involve the older, more experienced, person in supporting and engaging in discussions with the younger and often less experienced mentee. Both mentee and mentor would use the experience to facilitate reflection and discussion with the purpose of gaining an all-round education. It was explicit in these writings that the mentor supported the discussions with reflective and challenging questioning and would tend to hold back from handing out uninvited advice as has been suggested by, for example, Rosinski (2004).

more recent history

Daniel Levinson first presented the modern concept of mentoring in the USA in his (1979) book *The Seasons of a Man's Life*. This was a substantial longitudinal study of male development. Levinson used the term 'mentor' for someone, often half a generation older, who could help accelerate the development of another in his age-related transitions. He suggested that mentoring could reduce these age transitions from an average of seven to three years. This very quickly became the catalyst for a rapid growth in mentoring that would focus on an accelerated career progression in the USA.

In *Passages: Predictable Crises of Adult Life* (1976), Gail Sheehy discussed adult development mainly from a female perspective. At that time, she noted that mentoring relationships were not so common among women. However some twenty years later, in her revised edition, *New Passages: Mapping Your Life Across Time* (1996), she added developmental maps on both male and female development and noted that mentoring had become more common among women. She also noted a substantial social change in attitudes in both women's and men's lives in developed economies since her first edition had appeared in 1976. These changes were with regard to attitudes towards work, careers and equality.

Still in the USA, Kathy Kram has produced much good quality research on mentoring. This is discussed throughout the book but, in my view, her most significant contribution to the mentoring literature has been her statement that mentoring activity performs a *'psychosocial function'* (1983: 616); the mentee is socialised into a specific social context and develops self-insight and psychological wellbeing.

More generally within the mentoring literature there is a discussion around the psychological impact of mentoring. For example, Zaleznik (1977: 76) writes *'psychological biographies of gifted people repeatedly demonstrate the important part a mentor plays in developing an individual'*. He argues that leadership ability is developed through these intense and often intuitive relationships which have the affect of *'encouraging the emotional relationship leaders need if they are to survive'* (p. 78).

The theme of emotional development within mentoring is common and has its origins in history. Berman and West (2008: 744) show that mentoring activity increases the *'accurate awareness about one's emotional intelligence skills'* and many writers (Clawson, 1996; Levinson et al., 1978; Mullen, 1994; Smith, 1990; Zey, 1984) link a mentor's unconscious motivation to Erikson's (1978) psychological concept of 'generativity'. McAuley (2003) employs the psychological concepts of transference and countertransference in order to provide a deeper insight into the power dynamics that may be at play between mentor and mentee relationships. Garvey (2006) shows in two mentoring case studies that the intention for mentoring is not 'therapy' but its affect can be 'therapeutic'. In these cases, he links mentees' development to Levinson et al.'s (1978) framework of age-related transition and Jung's (1958) psychological concept of individuation.

These ideas seem to resonate with historical writings and bring together the idea that mentoring discussions play a role in cognitive, emotional and social development.

David Clutterbuck brought this modern concept of mentoring to the UK in 1983 with the publication of his book *Everyone Needs a Mentor*. This was a case study work inspired by David's experience in the USA. It is still in print and remains an all-time bestselling business book.

Many publications and a substantial body of research followed these milestones on both sides of the Atlantic and mentoring became established in developed economies.

According to Clutterbuck (2004) there are two main models of mentoring. In the USA, the emphasis is on *'career sponsorship'* whereas the European perspective is more *'developmental'* in approach, although there is some evidence (Kram & Chandler, 2005) that mentoring in the USA is changing to include a developmental approach.

Decades of US research also show that the *'sponsorship'* perspective brings with it many advantages for mentees, mentors and their host organisations. Carden (1990) and Allen et al. (2004) note that on the positive side, sponsorship mentoring activity can enhance knowledge, emotional stability, problem-solving, decision-making, creativity, opportunity, leadership abilities in individuals, and organisational morale and productivity.

In contrast, Ragins (1989, 1994); Carden (1990); Ragins and Cotton (1991); Ragins and Scandura (1999) indicate that mentoring with a career sponsorship orientation can be exclusive and divisive, encourage conformity among those with power, maintain the status quo and reproduce exploitative hierarchical structures. These elements can also lead to the relationship breaking down or becoming abusive.

In the UK, various studies (Clutterbuck, 2004; Garvey, 1995; Rix & Gold, 2000) demonstrate that *'developmental'* mentoring offers the same kind of positive benefits as identified within the US model but with fewer negative effects.

From the historical perspective, the issues that stand out in mentoring are:

- The social contexts of mentoring are important and influence the kind of mentoring that takes place.
- There is a common focus on career sponsorship or general and holistic development.
- The issue of experience and how it is used in the education of the mentees raises questions about the nature of advice giving.
- There are power dynamics within mentoring relationships.
- Mentoring seems to be consistently about change, transition and leadership.
- In some cases leadership is developed and in others it is demonstrated.
- It is largely a voluntary, emancipatory and speculative (Lyotard, 1984) developmental activity that can also be performative (Lyotard, 1984) over time.

a brief history of coaching

The term coaching appeared first in the English language in 1849 in Thackeray's novel, *Pendennis*. Set in nineteenth-century England, particularly in London, the main character, Arthur Pendennis, is a young English gentleman. Pendennis is born in the country and sets out for London to seek his place in life and society. The story offers an insightful and satiric picture of human character and the aristocratic society of the time.

The reference to coaching in the story is insubstantial and used as a play on words to describe both moving from A to B in a coach and to coach for academic attainment at Oxford University. Pendennis and his friends are travelling back to Oxford in a horse drawn coach and one says to the other *"I'm coaching there," said the other, with a nod. "What?" asked Pen, and in a tone of such wonder, that Foke burst out laughing, and said, "He was blowed if he didn't think Pen was such a flat as not to know what coaching meant." "I'm come down with a coach from Oxford. A tutor, don't you see, old boy? He's coaching me, and some other men ... "*

Other references to coaching in England during the same time describe:

- Tutoring for academic attainment.
- Improvement in performance in boating and rowing.
- Teaching defence of the wicket in cricket.

- Developing subject matter expertise, particularly in science.
- Teaching parenting skills.

These references, made in magazine articles or newspapers of the time, mainly discuss coaching as a group activity rather than a one-to-one activity. Some viewed coaching sceptically and even as unsporting, particularly with reference to the coach cycling on the towpath shouting instructions and advice to rowers on the river!

As far as I can discover, there are no works predating the nineteenth century devoted to exploring or describing the meaning and practice of coaching, therefore coaching, relative to mentoring, is a newer term. This does not mean, however, that coaching is a relatively modern concept. Some writers on coaching (Brunner, 1998; de Haan, 2008; Hughes, 2003) link it to classical times and especially Socratic dialogue.

Socratic dialogue is about the pursuit of self-knowledge and truth and is essentially a dialectic debate and inquiry between people of differing viewpoints. The Socratic approach takes widely held truths or dominant discourses that shape wider societal opinion and unpicks them to test their consistency with other beliefs. The Socratic method involves asking and answering questions to stimulate critical thinking and to illuminate ideas. It often involves an oppositional discussion in which the defence of one point of view is set against the defence of another. There is a sense of competition within the concept whereby one participant may lead another to contradict him in some way thus strengthening the inquirer's own point. The Socratic method identifies 'better' hypotheses by identifying and eliminating those hypotheses that lead to contradictions.

In my view, it is clear that elements of this method, such as asking questions and challenging ideas, are common features of modern coaching and mentoring practice. However, the approach was essentially a group and rather formalised, indeed almost ritualised, process. It is also, arguably, a negative methodology that has the potential to develop a cynical view of ideas and therefore could prove to be corrosive (Goldman, 1984; Kimball, 1986; Stone, 1988) rather than confirming. I will return to Socratic dialogue in Chapter 2.

There are some (McDermott & Jago, 2005; Zeus & Skiffington, 2000) who would also claim that coaching has been around since Stone Age times. The support offered for these claims is a narrative based on assumptions that early humans *must* have helped each other to improve at, for example, stone throwing or making axes. The interesting association here is that these writers are making *'performative'* links to coaching activity. With this in mind, some others (Starr, 2002; Wilson, 2007) suggest that coaching is derived from sport. Historical references from the nineteenth century support this idea, but perhaps more accurately the principles of academic coaching migrated, first, to rowing and then to cricket.

Many of the above writers also link the birth of modern business coaching to Timothy Gallwey's (1974) book *The Inner Game of Tennis*. This book is about the tennis player reaching a state of *'relaxed concentration'*. It presents a philosophy to enable players to discover their true potential. There is a strong psychological thread within the book as Gallwey explores the concepts of Self 1 (the teller) and Self 2 (the doer). In essence, Gallwey bases the philosophy on four steps:

1) Non-judgemental observation
2) Visualising the desired outcome
3) Trusting Self 2
4) Non-judgemental observation of change and results.

The overall concept of an 'inner game' offers an insight into the psychology of human performance and has resonances with various approaches to therapy, for example, psychodynamic, cognitive-behavioural, humanistic-existential, transpersonal and integrative-eclectic.

Following shortly after, Megginson and Boydell (1979) published a manual called *A Managers Guide to Coaching*. Here coaching is defined as *'a process in which a manager, through direct discussion and guided activity, helps a colleague to solve a problem, or to do a task better than would otherwise have been the case'* (p. 5). Coaching is here located in the workplace as a management activity.

A further milestone in coaching literature came in 1988 when Sir John Whitmore published *Coaching for Performance*. A central feature of this work is the GROW model and it is noteworthy that at least three people claim the development of GROW – Graham Alexander, John Whitmore, and Alan Fine. John Whitmore studied with Tim Gallwey, and as far as I can discover all four had contact with each other. The GROW model emphasises establishing the goal in coaching as a central feature. However, it is interesting to note that Gallwey is light on 'Goals' and 'Performance' discussions in his book. These issues are discussed later in Chapter 5.

Whitmore's book has since become an international bestseller and its contents are widely cited.

In terms of peer-reviewed research, the earliest seems to be Gorby's in 1937. This looked at coaching for waste reduction and profit enhancement. According to Grant and Cavanagh (2004: 5–6) *'Between 1937 and 1994, only 50 papers or PhD dissertations were citied in the PsychInfo and DAI databases. Between 1995 and 1999 there were 29 papers or PhD dissertations. Between 2000 and Nov 2003 there were*

49 citations. Between 1935 and Nov 2003 there were a total of 33 PhDs'.

They go on to summarise the content of these pieces as follows:

(a) discussion articles on internal coaching conducted by managers with direct reports;
(b) the beginnings of more rigorous academic research on internal coaching and its impact on work performance;
(c) the extension of research to include external coaching by a professional coach as a means of creating individual and organisational change;
(d) the beginning of coaching research as a means of investigating psychological mechanisms and processes involved in human and organisational change;
(e) the emergence of a theoretical literature aimed at the professional coach.

In summary, coaching seems to have emerged from several independent sources at the same time and spread through relationships and networks. This makes it a social activity. The intellectual frameworks seem to be a broad and eclectic mix, reflecting their social origins based on a cross-fertilisation of practices and different disciplines. Like mentoring, modern coaching practices are dynamic and contextual with coaching coming into existence to meet a variety of needs in a variety of situations. Common elements from the past indicate a discursive relationship aimed at an improvement in achievement within specific contexts, or in Lyotard's (1984) terms, 'performative' learning.

Its core roots are in:

- Education
- Sport
- Psychology and psychotherapy.

With subjects like philosophy and sociology influencing the discussions on coaching's meaning and contrary to current opinion, advice and teaching are elements from its history.

In a rather provocative article, Arnaud (2003: 1131–1132) states:

> After all, what does the entrepreneurial language in vogue today convey through its references to 'coaching' and 'coaches' if not the imagery of sports competition so cherished by management gurus (Berglas, 2002)? As such, the use of this terminology in the field of

> professional training can hardly be considered as neutral. The stereotypical image of the world-class athlete in training immediately comes to mind (Whitmore, 1994). Such an association not only flatters the ego of high-level managers/clients, it also gives a narcissistic boost to the coaches/trainers who supposedly dedicate body and soul to their noble and altruistic mission of making a success of their 'protégés'.

I discuss these issues, raised by Arnaud, throughout this book.

What really stands out for me is the almost relentless claim in the literature that coaching is an ancient and deeply embedded human activity. I think this is important. Making this claim is, in my view, evidence of the richly and socially constructed and diverse past of coaching. It is also speculative, associative and, arguably, takes history and rewrites it for the present. Perhaps on one level Nietzsche would approve, however, he was also concerned with honest questioning, however unpopular or contrary to the dominant discourse that might be.

So are these modern writers repositioning coaching and if they are what might their motives be?

Darwin (2010) provides an explanation and argues that 'truth' is an elusive concept. He employs the concept of 'alethic pluralism' to illustrate this. According to him (based on an analysis of the philosophies of Kuhn, Pooper, Feyerabend, and Lakatos), there are four possible ways in which something can be 'true' and these are neatly summarised below by Stokes (2010):

- Correspondence – what is said about a phenomenon must be true if it corresponds with what can be seen in the 'real' world.
- Coherence – what is said about a phenomenon must be true if the claims made seem plausible and internally consistent.
- Consensus – what is said about a phenomenon must be true if there is consensus between people about what it does.
- Pragmatism – what is said about a phenomenon must be true if it works/is practically adequate.

If we take the historical linkage for mentoring for example, there is evidence of the 'Correspondence' view of truth for mentoring in that the historical works do exist and these are relatively clear in their descriptions. Further, the 'Coherence' view of truth in the mentoring literature is contestable as these works seem to vary between their different contexts. The views from a 'Consensus' and 'Pragmatism' perspective are also contestable.

Taking the historical linkage for coaching, I contest the 'Correspondence' position because of the sheer variety of descriptions and associative linkage in the literature. Further, the 'Coherence' perspective is also variable as there are many descriptions of coaching in many contexts with many antecedents. The 'Consensus' position is also difficult to assess, as there are clearly many different groupings, approaches and contexts for coaching. What is clear is that some groupings have a 'Consensus' on what they believe to be true about coaching, for example, professional bodies. The 'Pragmatic' position may hold 'true' because many of those who write about coaching in a wide range of settings agree that it works!

Gibb and Hill (2006) and Clutterbuck and Megginson (2005: 15–17) suggest there are contrary positions presented in the coaching and mentoring literature that are almost 'tribal' in nature.

As a result of all this I would conclude that interest groups are offering different narrative lines based on the interests of their social groupings.

Garvey et al. (2009: 225) take these different sources of knowledge and practice in coaching and mentoring and bring them together in the following table.

Table 1.1 Antecedents, mediating concepts and practical applications for coaching and mentoring

Antecedents	Mediating concepts	Practical applications
Sport	Goals and targets Measurement Competitiveness Performance	GROW model Mental rehearsal Visioning Goal focus The inner game
Developmental psychology	Education theory Conversational learning theory Motivations Sense making Theories of knowledge Mindset The role of language Narrative theory Situated learning Adult development theories Age transitions	Levels of dialogue Holistic learning Knowledge productivity Johari's window

(Continued)

Table 1.1 *(Continued)*

Antecedents	Mediating concepts	Practical applications
Psychotherapy	Emotional disturbance Stress and wellbeing Blindspots and resistance to Change Transference Generativity Narrative theory Age transitions	7–eyed model of supervision CBT techniques Psychometrics Challenge Devil's advocacy Visioning Solution focus The dream The inner game Johari's window
Sociology	Organisational theory Relationships Change, power and emancipation Language, culture and context Dominant discourse Strategy Mindset Narrative theory	360° feedback SWOT and PESTS Performance management Human resource management practice ROI Discourse analysis
Philosophy	Power, morality and mindset Dominant discourses and meaning The notion of expert	Evidence-based coaching Existential coaching Ethical frameworks and standards

Source: Garvey et al. (2009: 225)

While this inevitably offers a single perspective on both coaching and mentoring, it also represents the diverse nature of the knowledge bases from which the activities are drawn as well as the sheer variety of practices. One result of this diverse and rich heritage is that different disciplines and philosophies find themselves in competition for the ownership of coaching and mentoring and I can only conclude that coaching and mentoring activities are socially constructed, dynamic and subject to reconstruction in various settings to suit a variety of purposes. Adding to this international and cultural considerations, there emerges a very mixed picture indeed.

A group of eminent coaching researchers and practitioners met in Dublin in 2008 for a global convention on coaching. From this they issued a declaration and their second point states:

> Acknowledge and affirm the multidisciplinary roots and nature of coaching as a unique synthesis of a range of disciplines that creates a new and distinctive value to individuals, organizations and society. To accomplish this we need to add to the body of coaching knowledge by conducting rigorous research into the processes, practices, and outcomes of coaching, in order to strengthen its practical impact and theoretical underpinnings. (Mooney, 2008: 5)

It would seem that there is support for the notion of an 'eclectic mix' in this statement and an acknowledgement that this would be achieved through rigorous research.

For me this raises a number of key questions – namely:

What are the implications of this eclectic mix on practice?
How do clients and consumers make informed choices?
What is good practice?
How is it possible to establish standards?
What's the difference between coaching and mentoring or are these the same?
How can coaching and mentoring be researched if there is no common definition?

I shall discuss these in the next chapter.

2

Are Coaching and Mentoring the Same? The Definition Debate

In this chapter I shall explore some of the current practice debates and research agendas and the importance of developing theory in coaching and mentoring by addressing the questions raised in Chapter 1:

- What are the implications of the eclectic mix discussed in Chapter 1 on practice?
- How do clients and consumers make informed choices?
- What is good practice?
- How is it possible to establish standards?
- What's the difference between coaching and mentoring or are these the same?
- How can coaching and mentoring be researched if there is no common definition?

In addition, I shall look at the diverse voices in coaching and mentoring and ask *'what is there to gain or lose by subscribing to a definitional approach?'*

introduction

In the last twenty years, the use of mentoring and coaching has gained momentum throughout industry, commerce and the public services (Bresser, 2008/9; Garvey, 1999).

The rapid rise in the utilisation of the coaching and mentoring has, in my view, led to two things: tremendous confusion and sometimes conflict about what the terms mean, and much posturing by and positioning of different interest groups. Therefore, among practitioners and academics alike, the quest for a true position is a bit like the *Coca Cola* versus Pepsi wars of the 1970s and 80s – is there a 'real thing' or is there an eclectic mix?

In Chapter 1, I referred to the Dublin Declaration (Mooney, 2008). Its first point states:

> Establish a common understanding of the profession through creation of a shared core code of ethics, standards of practice, and educational guidelines that ensure the quality and integrity of the competencies that lie at the heart of our practice. (2008: 5)

For me, this seems like a 'real' thing argument. The sentiments are clear and the intent is honourable, but how possible is this, particularly when taken in the context of the third statement in the declaration?

> Respond to a world beset by challenges for which there are no predetermined answers by using coaching to create a space wherein new solutions can emerge. In doing so we are stepping into the power of coaching as coaches and inviting our clients to do the same. (2008: 5)

It is the *'no predetermined answers'* element that interests me as it seems paradoxical to look for common understandings and shared positions if there are no predetermined answers because, in searching for common ground, there needs to be an assumption that such a ground exists! This point also mounts a challenge to the concept of 'goals' so commonly found in coaching and, to some extent, mentoring. So, are 'goals' predetermined positions (see Chapter 5)?

definitions in practice

I have recently engaged in an online debate about definitional issues with members of the European Mentoring and Coaching Council (EMCC). Its various participants are all well intentioned and united in wanting the best for coaching in particular and perhaps for mentoring also if they are pushed! I make this statement about their relationship with mentoring because most of these participants in the debate are from the commercial coaching sector and this inevitably brings with it the question raised in the introduction about the ethics of coaching with implications for mentoring. Despite the origins of the EMCC being in mentoring (it started life as the European Mentoring Centre), the number of people interested in mentoring has declined within the EMCC. This is possibly because the mentoring community is largely from the social and educational sectors. In these sectors, people almost exclusively view mentoring as a voluntary activity. I am not making this point in order to establish a higher moral authority for mentoring, as some others may choose to do, but to present a factual observation of the current marketplace. This is not to suggest that what might be called mentoring activity is declining; however, it is perhaps being repositioned or renamed as coaching!

A number of factors motivate professional bodies, for example:

- A unifying sense of direction in order to attract and keep members.
- A clearly articulated identity.
- Influence among its membership and among other stakeholders in order to become 'authoritative'.
- The need to establish standards, rules and regulations.

The EMCC definitional debate offered some interesting insights into the practical applications of alethic pluralism (as discussed in Chapter 1): for example, one participant used *'When applied to a real case ... '* as their opening line. This brief statement was an example of a 'Correspondence' view of truth. This contributor was, quite unwittingly, making an assumption that other cases might not be 'real' or that their sense of 'reality' was universal. As a lecturer in a university involved with management education, I experience this type of statement from managers regularly. It is as if their reality is the only possible reality, a positivistic and universal view of truth. Positivism operates using the following assumptions:

- Only phenomena and hence knowledge confirmed by the senses can genuinely be warranted as knowledge.
- The purpose of theory is to generate hypotheses that can be tested and will thereby allow explanations of laws to be assessed.
- Knowledge is arrived at through the gathering of facts that provide the basis for laws.
- Science must be conducted in a way that is value free.
- There is a clear distinction between scientific statements and normative statements and a belief that the former are the domain of the scientist. (Stokes, 2010: 3)

When applied to the EMCC definitional debate no-one would be participating because I do not believe that any participant in a professional body could genuinely claim to be neutral or value free. Further, coaching is, according to Brunner (1998: 516), *'... a domain devoid of any fixed deontology'*, and to some, though it has been more extensively researched, mentoring is undertheorised (Carmin, 1988). Added to this, the literature in coaching in particular is practice-based and consultant-led while in mentoring the literature is long on recommendations and checklists but short on locating practice within a framework of fundamental thinking, particularly about learning.

Moreover, definition in coaching and mentoring is, by definition, normative and not scientific! So where does all that leave us?

Another contributor stated: '... *an effort to find common ground* ...' This represents a 'Consensus' view of truth. Finding a common ground is a deeply embedded democratic position and gives rise to the statement '*if many agree, it must be true*'. In practice, it is also the philosophy behind trial by jury. However, could a minority voice be just as truthful or the majority be just plain wrong?

In some forms of research, for example medical research, there is a tendency to downgrade the minority voice in favour of the majority. This tends to develop an interesting new language or ciphers that will sideline or objectify the minority, for example, 'side effect' or 'contrary indication'. This is also a common issue with survey studies and seems to have become particularly prevalent in management language. Bauman (1989: 103) warns us of the consequences of this problem of objectifying:

> Reduced, like all other objects of bureaucratic management, to pure, quality-free measurements, human objects lose their distinctiveness. They are already dehumanized – in the sense that the language in which things that happen to them (or are done to them) are narrated, safeguards its referents from ethical evaluation. In fact, this language is unfit for normative-moral statements. It is only humans that may be objects of ethical propositions ... Humans lose this capacity once they are reduced to ciphers.

A democratically informed definition offers support to the 'regulatory principle'. This view of truth in relation to the EMCC has considerable merit as its intention is to reach a commonly agreed position. The reasons for this are due to the EMCC wanting European-wide acceptance and this means there is a need for a universal definition – the EU thinks in terms of a consensus truth!

While a consensus offers clarity for the majority, it can disempower or downgrade the minority as the majority view holds sway. Definition in social activities such as mentoring and coaching, if informed by a consensus view, therefore becomes a diversity issue.

Another contributor said '...' *it would be easier to approach the questions by using "dimensions" to find out where local understanding positions coaching. To explain the meaning of 'dimension' we provided the delegates with relevant literature ...*'

This is a 'Coherence' informed perspective in that it is attempting to build a plausible argument suggesting that the truth of a 'true' proposition consists of its coherence with some specified set of propositions. In this case what the literature says is likely to cohere with members' practical experience and therefore it becomes a true position. However, coherence theories of truth do not claim merely that coherence and consistency are important features of a theoretical system – they claim that these properties are 'sufficient' to its truth. In this way we end up with a 'good enough' position – which may have some merit provided the membership can live with 'good enough'.

The final comment made in this debate was *'Let us stay pragmatic ...'* Clearly, this is the pragmatic view of truth where, in simple terms, truth is what seems to work in practice. This also has an appeal for the practitioner, however, the sheer variation in practices and the claims made about them, perhaps influenced by self-interest or powerbases, means on a that agreeing on a definition becomes very difficult, even a pragmatic agreement. De Haan (2008) has an interesting position on this when he states that the choice of process model in coaching does not really matter much to the outcome but the quality of the relationship between coach and coachee does. Perhaps there is something to be gained here for the numerous authors of coaching process model books, including Blakey and Day (2009) who were discussed in the Introduction.

So once again, where does all this leave us? At a recent conference where I was presenting the above arguments there was a comment from the floor – *'It's all very well but executives like it simple.'* My response to this was – *'Yes, I agree that they do. However, running an organisation is a complex business and if, as executive coaches, we collude with the executive in their thought that all is simple, I would question the ethics of the coach's practice. I think it is better to try and engage with the complexity rather than collude with simplicity'.*

So what is the ethical position?

ethics in the coaching and mentoring debate

The first issue is management's mindset. Garvey and Williamson (2002) argue that the dominant mindset in western economies is one of pragmatic rationalism. Johnson and Duberley (2000) support this view when they claim that pragmatic positivism dominates management thinking and decision-making. The manager quoted above who wanted to keep things simple also reflects this position. This in turn links to both a Correspondence and a mainly Pragmatic view of truth. There is however a paradox here in that managers will often employ a 'Coherence' view of truth in order to make drastic changes to their organisations and a 'Consensus' view will only be used by management when this is convenient.

The literature claims that coaching and mentoring activity has the potential for creating a transformational change in people, for engaging with the complex and emerging with new insights. In general I have experienced such changes first hand and have also read accounts of this kind of experience. For me, there is another paradox here between the truth claims about transformational change made by practitioners and the mantra of keeping things simple. That is not to say that a transformational change is not simple. Sometimes it is, but despite this there remains the potential for a coach or mentor to collude with the simplicity agenda while denying that the topic under discussion is complex. Reducing the complex to something simple is potentially a form of denial and this also presents the potential for harm. Causing harm through this type of denial or collusion is unethical. It is also particularly paradoxical when the professed position for coaching and mentoring is to question and challenge at the same time as working with the coachee's/mentee's agenda!

To take another issue, as raised in Chapter 1, mentoring links directly to Ancient Greece and there are extant ancient writings that refer specifically to mentoring. If we look at probably the most common linkage to the ancients in coaching, Socratic dialogue, it is a hard to establish a truth position because the time lag and consequent reinterpretations over time make a direct link virtually impossible. If we add in Nietzsche's principle that studying history is potentially worthless unless we consider the context, we then have a major linkage problem to ancient history with both mentoring and coaching because our knowledge of the context of Ancient Greece is inevitably patchy and often speculative.

To look at modern descriptions of Socratic dialogue, according to Krohn (1998), we must recognise four key elements.

1. the concrete

The participants' discussion is within the context of their concrete and personal experiences. When the links between the concrete experience and the statements in the dialogue are made explicit, insight is achieved.

2. full understanding between participants

This involves more than a simple verbal agreement or explanation. The parties to the dialogue need to be clear about their meanings by testing them against their own concrete experience. In this way, limiting beliefs are explored in order for these to be transcended.

3. adherence to a subsidiary question until it is answered

Each participant in the dialogue needs to be committed to their work and develop self-confidence in the power of reason. This means being persistent in the face of challenge, as well as calm and humble enough to accept a different course in the dialogue in order to return to the subsidiary question. It is about honouring digressions while being persistent.

4. striving for consensus

Striving for consensus is more important than achieving consensus. It is primarily about honesty, trust and faith in the intent to reach a consensus through the examination of the thoughts of both self and others.

Taking a Coherence and Pragmatic view of truth, clearly there are many resonances in this explanation of Socratic dialogue within the historical and current practices in both coaching and mentoring. Additionally, a simple search on the internet shows that Socratic Coaching is widely used term that suggests a form of consensus. Further, there are many publications on the subject. For example, Neenan (2009: 249, 263) indicates that it is *'indispensable in the practice of coaching'* and *'an essential skill for all coaches to have as it encourages your coachees to reflect on their thinking and actions in order to develop new problem-solving perspectives, improve performance, achieve goals and take their lives in often unanticipated directions'*.

Neenan (2009: 250) states that Socratic coaching *'focuses on asking a person a series of open-ended questions to help promote reflection; this, in turn, is likely to produce knowledge which is currently outside of her awareness and thereby enable her to develop more helpful perspectives and actions in tackling her difficulties. Through this method people are able to reach their own conclusions rather than being told what these should be by the questioner'*.

However, I remain to be convinced that this is indeed Socratic questioning, specifically as Socrates intended, or that the linkage between the concrete and personal experiences should be made in order to develop insight. Arguably, the coach may point these out through a challenge if the coachee cannot make the links for his or her self. Additionally, there are no translations of Plato that use the term 'coaching' in relation to Socratic dialogue and therefore modern writers like Neenan (2009), de Haan (2008), Hughes (2003) and Brunner (1998) have made associative and not direct links to Socrates based on coherence arguments. Also, Socratic dialogue was about groups of people and not pairs as in coaching.

Further, to relate to another discipline more widely researched and studied than coaching, Socratic dialogue is a term used in education to describe a non-directive and critical approach to education, its fundamental purpose being to emancipate. Rud (1997: 2) argues that '... *Socratic teaching is taken to mean everything from dialectical examination of philosophical issues of justice, the good, and the like (Gray, 1988) to the use of questions by a teacher, independent of the subject matter (Kay & Young, 1986)*'. Moreover, Nietzsche was very challenged by the philosophical underpinning of Socratic dialogue and argued that Socrates' emphasis on painstaking rational analysis not only heralded the end of the vitality of Ancient Greece but also signposted the ending of creative mythology – the artistic interpretation driven out by rational analysis (this is discussed in Chapter 5).

Could Socrates be to blame for the current rational pragmatic mindset found in western management?! As a further challenge to Socratic dialogue, Nietzsche (1974: 206) stated '*One hears only those questions for which one is able to find answers*', suggesting that the Socratic way may not have taken human nature into account!

To develop this idea further, in a very challenging paper by Nielsen and Nørreklit (2009: 208) they take a quote from a respected and well reviewed and cited publication by Hunt and Weintraub (2002: 101): *"How did it go for you today?", "What did you see taking place?" and "What were you trying to accomplish?"*. They comment that this dialogue is '*staged, since the questioning is not aimed at enlightening the coach on specific issues. Instead, it is a meta-communicative means of controlling the coachee's capacity to respond*'. They conclude that '*this is a fake dialogue with questions anticipating stereotypical sets of answers*'.

To be fair, Hunt and Weintraub (2002) do not invoke Socratic dialogue anywhere in this publication – rather, it comes from Nielsen and Nørreklit (2009) – but Hunt and Weintraub (2002) do suggest that coaching is a management tool aimed at development. However, for me, the metaphor of 'tool' suggests control, manipulation, and an assumed power position. This type of alleged neutral questioning in the context of a manager as coach could be a form of surveillance that chimes with Foucault's (1979) concept of surveillance as an instrument of control. The coaching manager, by asking what seem to be supportive and innocuous questions, could be simply enacting a more acceptable form of control. I discuss this more in Chapter 3.

So what has led modern coaching writers to the link to Socrates? Without asking them, I can only speculate. Could this be another example of commercial positioning, as discussed in Chapter 1 and the Introduction? Is it the case that by giving a long historical association to coaching it gains more credibility? Could it be that linking coaching to Ancient Greece places it as a competitor to mentoring? Did the translators of Ancient Greek actually mean to talk about coaching but got the words wrong?

I am not saying that there is a deliberate intent here to mislead or rewrite history; however, what are the motivations behind these associative links? Are mentoring and coaching different activities or the same? Am I being pedantic to raise these issues and trying to complicate the 'simple' as my questioner suggested? I actually think I am doing my job as an academic, which is to critique, question and challenge, not for its own sake but in order to progress understanding, develop meaning and enhance practice – remembering, of course, that I am *for* mentoring and coaching.

I also do not think that there is anything too malicious here. There is energy, excitement and sometimes uncritical enthusiasm. However, there are also self-interests to be served and there could be something here about tackling a possible accusation that coaching is a new fad as well as an attempt to position it as something different from mentoring in order to differentiate it. Of more concern are the underdeveloped arguments or the lack of rigour in the 'research' used to make the historical link. There is a plethora of these claims but is it perhaps that the writers are either quoting each other or writing what they believe to be true because it is part of a dominant social narrative?

Applying the 'truth test' to claims made about coaching and mentoring offers some basis for critical thought and, as Darwin (2010) suggests, the likelihood of a 'truth' being established is increased if more than one truth position is satisfied.

addressing definitional questions

To return to the questions raised at the start of this chapter –

- What are the implications of the eclectic mix discussed in Chapter 1 on practice?
- How do clients and consumers make informed choices?
- What is good practice?
- How is it possible to establish standards?
- What's the difference between coaching and mentoring or are these the same?
- How can coaching and mentoring be researched if there is no common definition?

An eclectic mix offers a challenge to most of the issues raised by the above questions. Professional bodies, commercial businesses and researchers mostly require clarity and precision in order to do their work. These groupings present themselves to specific social sectors and therefore they need to reflect the mindsets of the specific sector if they are to have appeal. Arguably, this could become a piece of mass, localised, uncritical collusion! The EMCC has difficulty in maintaining the educational and voluntary elements of its membership and consequently also has a problem in maintaining its mission. Definition would provide focus but it would also exclude. The expanding market and commercialisation of coaching, and to some extent mentoring, fuels the debate and energises the search for the 'real thing' rather than the acceptance of an eclectic mix. Schon (1983: 7) commented *'On the high ground, management problems lend themselves to solution through the application of research based theory and technique. In the swampy lowland, messy confusing problems defy technical solution'.*

As discussed in Chapter 1, both mentoring and coaching share similar skills, processes and intents and the arguments for difference are often related to the context, whether it is paid or voluntary, and the view taken on the use of 'experience' by the coach or mentor. On this basis, it would appear that there is the potential for a consensus view, but there are vested interests here which mean that there are 'power' positions to defend. I discuss this in Chapter 3.

As for research, definition is one position in research philosophy. Coaching and mentoring are, in my view, in the *'swampy lowlands'* and while it is important for researchers to clearly describe the social phenomenon they are researching in order to differentiate it from another, definition is not the only way because it is in essence reductionist and simplifying. In a world of increasing complexity, simplicity has an appeal. However, the sheer variety of practice, context and intent within the worlds of coaching and mentoring means that it is probably more appropriate to work towards a rich and *'thick description'* (Geertz, 1971) of mentoring and coaching in as many different forms as possible to highlight their complexity rather than attempt to simplify this. In such a way, we may reach a state of tolerance with the eclectic mix and become emancipated (Lyotard, 1984) rather than oppressed by the shackles of the powerhouse of the 'real' thing argument where he who has the power dominates. As Layder (1994: 97) states:

> ... it is important to understand that language is never 'innocent'; it is not a neutral medium of expression. Discourses are expressions of power relation and reflect the practices and the positions that are tied to them. A discourse here refers to all that can be thought, written or said about a particular thing such as a product (like a car, or a washing detergent), or a topic or specialist area of knowledge (such as sport or medicine). In this sense, the ability to employ a discourse reflects a

> command of knowledge of a particular area. It also implies that this facility is employed in relation to people who lack such command and have no legitimate claim to such knowledge. For instance, command of a particular discourse, such as that of medicine or law, also allows control over those who do not, such as patients and clients.

Discourses are important shapers of behaviour in societies as McAuley et al. (2007: 265) suggest:

> Discourses are sets of ideas and practices that condition our ways of relating to and acting upon particular phenomena; a discourse is expressed in all that can be thought, written or said about a particular topic, which by constituting the phenomena in a particular way, influences behaviour.

Chapter 3 explores discourse of power and asks where the dominant discourses in coaching and mentoring are and where this might lead us.

3

What are the Discourses and What are We Not Hearing in Coaching and Mentoring?

This chapter explores the discourses of the different contexts in which coaching and mentoring activity takes place. It considers the power bases of the professional bodies and the established networks for coaching and mentoring and asks the question *'what roles and functions do coaching and mentoring activities perform within a shifting social and economic context around the world?'*

introduction

The Dublin Declaration of 2008 attempted to address the issue of power-bases in its fourth point where it stated:

> Move beyond self-interest and join with us and other members of the Global Coaching Community in an ongoing dialogue to address the critical issues facing our field ... (Mooney, 2008: 5)

This is another powerful acknowledgement of the challenges facing the coaching world in particular, but by implication the mentoring world as well.

The concept of dominant discourse is of central importance both to cultural determination and to power structures in society, because as Webster (1980: 206) states *'Language is the primary motor of a culture ... Language is culture in action'*. The way we talk, the language we use and the metaphors and similes we utilise create meaning. These meanings shape beliefs, actions and behaviours. As raised in previous chapters, social groups are shaped by narratives and the language of each narrative creates, sustains, develops and changes the culture. The dominant language tends to be the one that holds sway, it is the power position.

This point is beautifully illustrated in George Orwell's *Animal Farm*. In this story, the pigs take, shape and maintain control and change the power positions through slogans – *'all animals are equal'* becomes *'but some are more equal than others!'*, and *'two legs bad, four legs good'* changes to *'two legs good, four legs bad'* as the pigs begin to stand up. Politicians of today know this well as do marketing and advertising people. The writer Salman Rushdie, who was forced into hiding with extensive police protection following the publication of his book, *The Satanic Verses*, expresses this very point in the following extract.

> Those who do not have the power of the story that dominates their lives – power to retell it, rethink it, deconstruct it, joke about it, and change it as times change – truly are powerless because they cannot think new thoughts. (Rushdie, 1991)

There is also a time dimension to all this. I have already raised the issue of history as a shaper of the present and informer of the future in Chapter 1. Time is an inescapable dimension of human experience and any satisfactory account of how an organisation (and the people within it) works must attend to the ways in which lives are changing constantly and are constructed in time. The past is often remembered through stories and these stories form part of the dominant discourse.

According to Bruner (1990), people shape meaning from the past through narrative, metaphor and stories. Often, in an organisational setting, the perspective we have on the past will be influenced by the dominant via narrative and communicated through the holders of that power. Karl Marx (1852) gave us an insight into this:

> Men make their own history, but not of their own free will; not under circumstances they themselves have chosen but under the given and inherited circumstances with which they are directly confronted. The tradition of the dead generations weighs like a nightmare on the minds of the living.

This is a very challenging statement and one which is laden with ethical questions, responsibilities and commitments and for me, an opportunity for change.

My position here is that human 'pasts' are actually constantly in our 'presents' but we are not often aware of this as we simply 'get on' with our lives. There will be times when the 'past' confronts our 'present' and this will tend to happen during 'moments' of awareness, significance or critical insight. I believe that people do have choices but that this in itself is not straightforward.

possible positions on discourse

For me, there are three possible positions within the area of discourse:

Position 1 is where we may decide to live in the past and function using traditionalism. This has the effect of making people resistant to change because the basic reference point for action in the present is traditionalism. This creates a sense of security – that there is an answer in history and all we have to do is simply repeat it and things will be alright! The tacit assumption here is that everything people do in an uncritical celebration of the past is known, controllable and predictable. This is despite a strongly held perception that while the organisation may feel itself to be 'modern', the tried and trusted paths dominate.

Position 2 is where we may choose to reject our past or re-write our history. This has the potential effects of devaluing our past and making it worthless or we may apportion blame, attach guilt or have a 'rose-tinted' perspective on our history. This attitude often prevents people in organisations from learning from the past or encourages them to suppress its continuing influence on their present-day actions. In my view this is a very negative position and one that I have directly experienced: the dominant slogan perpetuated by one new boss who was trying to change the organisation to have it focus on a different way of working was *'undergraduate good, postgraduate bad!*

Position 3 is one which attempts to build on our past by understanding it profoundly. We do this through an adequate reflection on our past and a critical awareness of our past. This requires openness and a willingness to be critical, to learn and to change. It invites people to take risks – with their reputations, status and careers. For some it will be a painful realisation that cherished beliefs were misplaced, that previous attitudes were unhelpful. One way to think about this is to consider the idea of significant moments of change in our lives. Obviously these can often be understood only in retrospect. And, as time changes, our perception of moments and significant turning points may alter. How people talk about and analyse critical moments in organisational history is often a real clue about the defining character of an organisation's culture or an individual's character, attitudes and behaviours. This for me is the domain of coaching and mentoring. This position does not provide easy options but in my view it is necessary to confront the past in this way, otherwise it becomes our prison. I shall raise Position 3 arguments again in Chapter 4.

In the workplace defining 'moments' do happen but, as Marx indicated in the previous quote, we cannot control these 'moments' we can only choose our response to them.

In today's global working environment the opportunities which present themselves for scrutiny are unknowable, complex and often happen quickly. As raised earlier, people tend to respond to these 'moments' by referencing their past. As we cannot predict from where and when these 'moments' will happen, we can only prepare for our response by understanding our past. I often consider the slogan *'chance favouring the prepared mind'* in this context. For me, the 'prepared mind' is one that is open to ideas and critically reflective and reflexive and I would speculate that the third position outlined above offers the most potential for individuals and organisations to realise a positive future that does not repeat the failings of the past. Position 3 contains profound implications for coaching and mentoring. For organisations to realise their futures they need to critically understand their 'pasts' because these are the backdrop for actions and decision-making. An organization's past is remembered through the dominant narratives within its culture and it seems to me that there can be various versions of these narratives and that understanding each one offers us an informed choice. In both the coach and mentoring literature developing and exploring the many options for action is a core discourse (e.g. Clutterbuck & Megginson, 2005; Dembkowski & Eldridge, 2003; Garvey, 2006; Phillips, 1996).

the mentoring discourses

As discussed in the previous two chapters, definition in mentoring and coaching is problematic but by examining definitional statements, it is possible to gain some insight into the narrative that gave the definition life. For example:

> Mentoring is a one-to-one, non-judgemental relationship in which an individual voluntarily gives time to support and encourage another. This is typically developed at a time of transition in the mentee's life, and lasts for a significant and sustained period of time. (Active Community Unit, Home Office, UK)

This definition has a social context in mind – the community. It emphasises 'non-judgemental' 'voluntary', 'support' and 'encourage' as key qualities and behaviours within the relationship. It also places an element of timeliness within it and indicates that this relates to personal development changes. This definition positions mentoring within a context and therefore it is a guiding and almost instructional statement that hopes to shape the activity. The holders of power here were the UK Home Office. This is significant for in 2001 the then Chancellor of the Exchequer, Gordon Brown, was investing a total of £13million in youth mentoring schemes across the UK. The fast food chain McDonalds also financed the initiative. This act of alleged generosity on behalf of McDonalds could of course have had many different and conflicting interpretations that would link it to the discourses of commercial and social power and perhaps the more cynical among us may have had some questions about the motivation for such an act!

Governments do not invest money without the expectation of a social return. Social mentoring activity was a concept borrowed by the British government from the USA. Freedman (1999), in relation to the 'Big Brothers and Big Sisters' youth mentoring scheme there, described it as *'fevor without infra-structure'*. He argued that government-funded youth mentoring had a strong political driver that tapped into the middle-class US fears of the 'underclass' and provided a 'quick fix' to social problems. In his view, it produced a *'heroic conception of social policy'* (p. 21) that invited middle-class Americans to undertake a 'crusade' to save the often Black and Latino underclass. Other studies (e.g. Grossman & Tierney, 1998) do suggest that youth mentoring in the USA makes a positive difference to the mentee but that mentors who focused on the goals prescribed by the scheme or funders rather than on the person had much less success. Colley (2003) found the same in her studies in the UK.

However, policy makers will often ignore some of the cautionary statements from research. The question of whose agenda is being played out in government-sponsored schemes is part of the discourse of power. The arguments are not necessarily based on any form of 'truth' position (see Chapters 1 and 2), but perhaps as Garmezy (1982: xix) points out on a *'false sense of security in erecting prevention models that are founded more on values than on facts'* or on ideological or political reasons.

If we take another definition from the social sector of mentoring, we can find a different emphasis.

> ... support, assistance, advocacy or guidance given by one person to another in order to achieve an objective or several objectives over a period of time. (SOVA)

SOVA is a UK-based voluntary organisation that works within communities to help strengthen them and reduce crime. This definition also attempts to shape the mentoring relationship. It emphasises certain activities and functions and also adds in the concept of objectives, arguably drawn from the managerial discourse. Perhaps SOVA employ this managerial discourse of 'targets' in an attempt to appeal to UK government funding criteria for voluntary sector mentoring.

Looking to other countries, Zey (1984: 7) in the USA defines a mentor as: '*a person who oversees the career and development of another person usually a junior, through teaching, counselling, providing psychological support, protecting, and at times promoting and sponsoring. The mentor may perform any or all of the above functions during the mentor relationship*'.

This definition has a different emphasis to the previous two and places the mentor in a power position as they 'oversee' someone 'junior' and the mentor clearly performs some specific functions to achieve career progression. This view of mentoring chimes with Clutterbuck's (2007) position that there are two main models of mentoring as mentioned in Chapter 1. Some (e.g. Megginson et al., 2005) have argued that the purpose of the mentoring influences the design of the scheme and may have the affect of highlighting or reducing the negative impact of power dynamics.

To examine some of the discourses as presented by different countries for executive mentoring for example, Clutterbuck and Megginson produced the following table that shows a variety of culturally led discourses in mentoring:

Table 3.1 Characteristic approaches to executive mentoring by country

Country	Goals	Style of relationship	Features in scheme
USA	Sponsorship Promoting career	Paternalistic	Senior director taking up cause of younger high flyer
France	Insight Analysis of life purpose	Commitment to sharing values	Scheme created outside companies
Netherlands	Mutual support Learning Networking	Informal Egalitarian Peer mentoring Universal	Recognising benefits for mentor and mentee Personal and professional
Sweden	Perpetuate culture	Share understanding Exchange knowledge	Strong sponsorship from HR and CEO
Britain	Insight Learning Support	Individualistic, charismatic mentor shares insights and challenges mentee	Ad hoc Diversity of opportunities

Source: Clutterbuck and Megginson (1999: 140)

Different purposes, underpinned by different definitions, will create different narratives, which in turn will create different dominant discourses, all of which will influence practice.

As was raised in Chapter 1, Kram (1983: 616) states that mentoring performs a psychosocial function and current practice suggests that this is the case in the UK – however, I have recently noticed a change in that more organisations are starting to link mentoring activity to 'talent' management and leadership development in the same way that the US model has developed. Where this will eventually take us is difficult to assess right now.

the coaching discourses

To take the same approach as the mentoring section, here are some definitions of coaching.

> The art of facilitating the unleashing of people's potential to reach meaningful, important objectives. (Rosinski, 2004: 4)

In unpicking this definition, Rosinski places 'objectives' as a primary focus and suggests that *'Coaching is oriented toward concrete impact and results'*. To me, this is a discourse intended to appeal with the business world or the 'pragmatic' truth discourse (see Chapter 2). I think that Rosinski intends that *'meaningful, important'* are linked with the coachee, but they could be equally linked to what is meaningful or what is understood to be meaningful to the coach or host organisation. Linking *'meaningful'* to the coachee is a very common discourse in coaching texts. Stated another way, it is referred to as the coachee's agenda and this is generally seen as the primary driver for coaching. The *'unleashing'* could suggest that the person is in a kind of captivity, tethered to something perhaps, and this implies that the coach is offering to 'facilitate', or in Rosinski's (2004: 5) words, he or she *'enables coachees'*. There could be an assumption here that the coachee needs enabling because they may be disabled themselves and the process of *'enabling'* gives power to the coach. He goes further with the power being in the hands of the coach when he states *'Great coaches often have a vision of what that potential might be'*. For me, this really does place the power with the coach because the statement assumes that they are endowed with greater 'vision'. I view this as a somewhat patronising view of the coachee. However, it may indeed be the case in the discourse of sport that a coach may indeed have greater vision – this is certainly referred to in the media and may be a contributing factor in the generally rapid turnover of, say, soccer coaches around Europe. It may also link to the idea that coaches may be able to spot someone's potential and then develop it. (See Arnaud (2003), quoted in Chapter 1.)

Some years ago I worked for a consultancy company, the MaST Organisation, and we hosted an event called 'Motivation for Results'. One of our guest speakers was top coach Tom McNab. Tom coached Daley Thompson, the two times Olympic gold medal winner and four times world record holder for the decathlon, regarded by many as the greatest decathlon athlete ever. Many attributed Daley's success to being 'spotted' by Tom. When asked about this, Tom had replied that he had first seen Daley when he was a boy and noticed he could run very fast. He said that he gave him his first pair of running shoes and created the environment – the national junior decathlon programme – and that Daley did the rest. Tom may have been very modest or could this have been an acknowledgement of the serendipitous nature of 'talent spotting'? It could have also indicated that 'environment' plays an important part in the development of talent. There was no doubt that Daley was talented but was it Tom who 'unleashed' this or would Daley have done that for himself?

taking another typical definition

> ... coaching is a conversation or a series of conversations, one person has with another. The person who is the coach intends to produce a conversation that will benefit the other person (the coachee) in a way that relates to the coachee's learning and progress. Coaching conversation might happen in many different ways in many different environments. (Starr, 2008: 4)

This definition emphasises the conversation between two people. The '*coach intends*' seems to suggest that the conversation is led by the coach and therefore the power lies with that coach. However, the conversation is for the benefit of the coachee's learning and progress and so this is another example of the coachee's agenda being central. This definition suggests that the context for these conversations is the variable here. For me the emphasis is on the coach – the notion that it is for the coachee's own good implies patronage on behalf of the coach. I have heard experienced coaches suggesting on many occasions that they have the ability to change a person's behaviour or attitude. But there seems to be a paradox with this view – the coaching is about the coachee's agenda but the coach has the power to change things despite being agendaless – all very curious!

a third definition

> Coaching is a pragmatic approach to helping people manage their acquisition or improvement of skills. (Clutterbuck, 1998: 19)

This definition emphasises the '*pragmatic*' acquisition and development of skills and, for me, places coaching within the management discourse of 'utility' and 'performative' knowledge (Lyotard, 1984; see Chapter 1) and this offers a clearly different definition to the previous ones offered above – one that is aligned with a management discourse.

bringing things together ...

The definitions presented here on both mentoring and coaching emphasise four basic elements in four different ways as follows:

1) The role of the mentor or coach.
2) Client expectations.
3) The purpose or intended outcomes for mentoring and coaching.
4) The context or boundaries of the mentoring and coaching encounter.

the role

For some, the role of the coach or mentor is to facilitate the conversation by employing skills such as counselling, listening and questioning and the coach or mentor must possess certain personal attributes that will enable them to be helpful, supportive and guiding.

client expectations

The client's expectations will often be implied from the language they use. It can also be difficult to know who the client is in some cases! This could be the coachee or mentee but it could also be the commissioner of the service or a manager. Generally, the expectation will be that the intervention will be helpful and achieve something. The concept of 'power' is underplayed here but this is a false assumption in that all the discourses expressed above have elements of power within them.

purpose

Some definitions specifically raise the issue of objectives and often place these with the coachee or mentee. This is despite the sponsors having a clear purpose for investing in the coaching or mentoring activity. These purposes can be learning and development, but they can also be linked to performance improvement, change, career progression, gaining employment, and in some cases, a compliance (though this is never stated) with social norms.

contexts

Many definitions are not context specific and, like the purpose and expectations elements, offer contextual information by implication. However, different contexts as discussed earlier will produce different discourses and as a result, if a coaching or mentoring arrangement is to be successful, the definition needs to relate to the discourse of the context for which it is intended.

so what?

This is an interesting question! The challenges posed by competitive context in the modern world, dominated by the capitalist doctrine, give rise to discourses that offer a variety of versions of the 'real world'. These discourses influence and affect all of us both socially and economically. How we respond to these 'worlds' at various moments will depend on the dominant narrative and the way this is interpreted through the dominant discourse – namely, the ways in which people talk to each other.

If, for example, the narrative is dominated by a pragmatic manager or is dominated by the 'technical' perspective, decisions will be made against this pragmatic/technical backdrop and any alternative perspective may not be considered. This is not to denigrate the pragmatic perspective – this can often be very helpful – but it may not offer the best opportunity for learning because the lens through which ideas are examined is unitary rather than pluralist. As I showed in Chapters 1 and 2, there are contexts and multiple discourses involved and these can be used to aid our understanding of the complexities of the coaching and mentoring worlds though critical reflection. This will obviously result in alternative options being expressed.

It is interesting to note that Clutterbuck, one of the most prolific and respected writers on coaching and mentoring in the last twenty years, has changed his views on the meaning of coaching and mentoring. Together with Megginson, a writer and researcher of similar standing, they have both acknowledged that '*We have recently produced a model that demonstrates how practitioners in both fields have tried to claim the facilitative end of the developmental spectrum for themselves, while denigrating the other by placing it at the directive end. We argue that this strategy is futile ... we have been as guilty as many other writers of engaging in these shenanigans (Megginson & Clutterbuck, 1995; Clutterbuck and Megginson, 1999)* (Clutterbuck & Megginson, 2005: 14).

This is an honest acknowledgement of the power dynamics within the activities of coaching and mentoring. The power struggles will no doubt continue but what of the voices that are not being heard?

the unheard voices

While writers will position themselves as a result of various motivations and engage in power discourses, many people will engage with coaching and mentoring and simply 'get on with it'. These groups also have a discourse but one that is often not heard above the noise of the dominating groups.

Helen Colley (2003), in her book *Mentoring For Social Inclusion: A Critical Approach to Nurturing Relationships,* points out that in government-funded social mentoring schemes there are often elements of '*unacknowledged power dynamics at work such as, class, gender, race, disability, sexuality that may either reduce or reproduce inequalities*' (p. 2). This, allied with the often tightly specified outcomes imposed by the funders, can lead to negative outcomes and an exacerbation of the very problems that the intervention was supposed to resolve. So, for example, a discourse of '*formal, paid employment is good, unemployment is bad*' when applied to the third generation of unemployed in an environment where this is the norm, makes any mentoring intervention that does not engage with the mentee's discourse of '*unemployment is normal*' fatuous and patronising. She suggests, in a similar fashion to Foucault (1979), that such concepts are socially constructed: '*It may be more effective and less stressful for those involved in mentoring to think of social exclusion as a process that society imposes on its most disadvantaged members, rather than as a set of characteristics attributed to them*' (p. 176). In other words, 'exclusion' is not a factual, rational position; it is defined by a dominating discourse in society. It remains a matter of opinion!

In the coaching world, and particularly in the context of business, one discourse revolves around performance and goals. Coaches may assume that this is what managers want and managers may assume that this is what they will get. We rarely hear the coachee's voice in all this. If we take a situation where the coach is a paid professional, for example, it can be difficult to establish the nature of the relationship and identifying precisely who the client might also be challenging. Is the client the person who commissions the work? How much voluntarism is there from the coachee's perspective? Is the client the person who pays for the service? Or could it be the coachee? It is my experience that these questions can potentially raise conflicts of interest.

A colleague of mine, as an external coach, was put under considerable pressure to reveal his coachee's objectives to the HR manager who had commissioned the coaching work. My colleague responded by suggesting that the coachee was the one who should be asked this and not him – a reasonable enough position given the discourse of the coachee's agenda to which he subscribed! The HR manager persisted but my colleague held firm, stating that he had a confidentiality agreement with his coachee. The manager retorted that he was paying for the coaching and thus had a right to know.

Clearly, there were power dynamics at play here and a discourse of control on the agenda. In relation to the performance issue my colleague had been commissioned to work with, the coachee did not see it in the same way as either the HR manager or his own manager who had requested the intervention. However, his voice was not heard in all this and the coach was left to deal with an issue that, in my view, the coachee's manager should have dealt with himself.

I think this is a common experience – multiple agendas at work, multiple discourses, expectations and interpretations, at the same time as all the parties involved believing that it was all about the coachee – except, of course, the disempowered coachee who eventually got so fed up with the discourse that he moved to a competing employer on a much higher salary! Now they have to deal not only with a competitor but also with a competitor who has passionate desire for revenge!

In this case, 'performance' was defined by the dominant discourse of the organisation and no account was taken of the coachee's position – his discourse, about prejudice, victimisation and harassment, went unheard. They had brought in an external coach to 'fix' him without engaging in the kind of critical reflective discussion raised in Position 3 at the start of this chapter. The issue of performance is discussed in Chapter 5.

Another strongly established discourse in coaching and mentoring exists around the issue of 'goals'. In the coaching literature, the discourse of goals is embedded in the coaching process model GROW – the most commonly used model for coaches (http://www.the-coaching-academy.com/life-personal-performance-coaching/articles/GROW-model.asp). In the mentoring literature it is less firmly established but nonetheless discernable – for example, Garvey and Alred (2001: 523) state:

> Mentoring is an activity that addresses a combination of short, medium and long term goals, and concerns primarily 'ends' as well as 'means'.

Research (Megginson, 2007) suggests that 'goals' are not necessarily a preoccupation for all people and that those who do not subscribe to the dominant discourse of 'goals' can still have a sense of direction and intent in their work and lives. However, summarising Megginson (2007: 48) below, the problem with 'goals' is that they can:

- Create conflict between the client's goals and the intent of the organisation.
- Over-target people and pileing on goals in their leadership roles is just counterproductive.
- Oversimplify the relationship and lead to a superficial and circumscribed dialogue.
- Become instruments of control rather than motivators.
- Become downright destructive and obsessive.

Additionally, there is always more than one way to achieve a goal! Goals that are not grounded in what needs to be achieved and how this is to be achieved are always problematic.

A further discourse, particularly in mentoring, is focused on the concept of altruism. Research from one UK public sector organisation (Garvey, 1998) that introduced mentoring showed that there was no problem in finding volunteers to become mentors but there was a grave shortage of potential mentees. Many of these volunteers were well intentioned and had great potential to be very good mentors. However, the strong hierarchy and status orientation, which characterised the organisation, meant that becoming a mentor was also a confirmation of status. Seemingly influenced by the discourse of altruism, which is often associated with mentoring, these mentors expressed their desire to take part in order 'to put something back' into the organisation. This is a commonly found motivation and on the surface, one which seems reasonable, but in this particular context it was more about the potential mentors' insecurity in the face of reorganisation and change than about 'putting something back'. In some ways, this 'putting back' can represent a form of arrogance on the part of a potential mentor. It is about *them* and their contribution rather than the mentee's development and this may lead to the mentoring function being based on advice-giving – a common discourse from coaches writing about mentoring!

The lack of potential mentees coming forward was perhaps a sign that the mentees had fears and concerns about mentors' motivations. Consequently, they sought developmental support outside of the mentoring scheme. Mentoring was thus working in the 'shadows' (Egan, 1993). Mentoring does occur naturally outside of a formal scheme and sometimes this is just as effective and legitimate as the formal process (see Ragins & Cotton, 1999). According to Egan (1993), *'shadow-side'* is what happens unofficially in an organisation. It is about conversations and actions behind the scenes well away from the overtly managed. He argues that this shadow-side is unmanageable and has the potential to add value or take it away and that it is a function of the culture in an organisation. Egan suggests that in a controlled, bureaucratic hierarchy a destructive shadow-side is more likely to be the case.

Clutterbuck (2004) advocates that in a mentoring scheme design, the mentor should not be the line manager because of the potential conflicts of interest and the potentially inappropriate power dynamics. Garvey (2005) presented a case study where the management in the organisation developed a mentoring programme that was intended to be the main driver of cultural change. The line managers were also the mentors. The existing cultural pressures meant that the scheme slipped into the 'shadow-side' where it worked against senior and distant managerially-led changes as mentors and mentees colluded to maintain the status quo. It is interesting to note that this organization stopped the mentoring scheme, re-branded it, and launched it again as a coaching scheme with a new discourse of 'performance enhancement'! A key point here is that the fundamentals of the culture were not addressed by either mentoring or coaching in part because it was the same people taking on the role of either 'mentor' first time round or 'coach' the second. Another element was that the organisation adopted the discourses of both mentoring and coaching and assumed that these were different activities, but at the same time they were unable to address core issues within a long history of misuse of power and fractured relationships within the business. They expected that mentoring and after that coaching would address these problems.

In another organisation a mentor said – *'mentoring enables me to spread my influence around the organization, it gives me allies'.* Although this may have been true and could have been seen as positive for the mentor, this comment was also about establishing a political power base rather than a developmental alliance for the mentee.

The issue of 'line manager as coach or mentor' is also a developing discourse. There are a number of reasons for this. In the current declining and very nervous economic climate, despite claims in the coaching press to the contrary (e.g *Coaching at Work*, July 2009; Nov 2009; Jan 2010), my sense of the current market for external coaching is that it is getting tougher. I have based this on conversations with coaching colleagues and within my organizational networks. On the other hand, the development of line manager as coach is becoming more prevalent (e.g. *Coaching at Work*, June 2009; Nov 2010), perhaps in order that organisations can gain the benefits of coaching without the high costs of employing an external coach. A further question to consider here is *'where is the voice of the coachee?'* in all this? I think that there are lessons for coaching to learn here from mentoring's experience.

According to Alred and Garvey (2010: 92), success in mentoring schemes is often associated with two main factors:

- The visible participation of senior managers as mentors and mentees.
- Starting small and growing gradually, stimulated by enthusiasm and positive example, and organisational support.

Another issue is the question of choice and voluntarism and this links to how people are matched together. Both experience and research have shown that the way people are put together in mentoring pairs can affect the outcomes. Matching for both similarity and difference has potential benefits and a good match will attend to the contrasts and differences between mentee and mentor, as well as any similarities.

In my work with developing coaching managers, I have come across many organising arrangements for putting people together. For example:

- Line manager as coach to individual team members.
- Line manager as coach to the whole team together.
- Cross-functional or inter-departmental coaches.
- Cross-functional, inter-departmental coaches where a line manager provides the agenda for coaching.

As with mentoring schemes, the potential for power dynamics to influence the discussion is always present within coach-manager arrangements, but the cross-functional or inter-departmental arrangements with the coachee holding the agenda do seem to hold the promise of reducing power problems.

McClelland and Burnham (1976) do not see the application of *'socialized power'* as something that is necessarily associated with *'dictatorial behaviour'*, but as *'a desire to have an impact, to be strong and influential'* (p. 235). This type of power, which they associate with the *'good manager'*, is not focused on the individual and *'personal aggrandizement'* (p. 235), instead it is aimed *'toward the institution which he or she serves'* (p. 235). McClelland and Burnham suggest that the successful manager is one who is able to use *'socialized power'* for the benefit of the organisation. I remember presenting this argument to an academic audience in the past and the polite version of the comments I received was *'rubbish'!* They may have had a point!

Power may be described in terms of the attributes held by the majority in an organisation. This is influenced by the organisation's structure and values. Personal power is more associated with a charismatic leader but this influence is often transitory in nature and short term. Mentoring and, to some extent, coaching activity is usually more long term than this (Levinson et al., 1978). Arguably, the 'good' mentor or coach will have the needs of the organisation in his or her mind (although there are no guarantees here) and the whole picture, as well focusing their attention on the needs of the individual. Mentoring and coaching focused in this way, potentially at least, can create a unique and special relationship that works. De Haan (2008) in his book *Relational Coaching* goes further when he emphasises the need for a strong trusting relationship to develop as this is the key to coaching success. However, recent events in the Banking sector suggest that very high rewards distort behaviours more towards *'personal aggrandizement'* than the organization and I do wonder if people really are capable of genuine altruism in a capitalist economy.

As raised in the Introduction and Chapter 2, the rational, pragmatic manager often has an agenda of control. This is usually presented in the form of a performance management system. This is discussed more in Chapter 5, but in my view performance is a function of the environment that is created – managers can make it more or less possible for people to perform well by the way they interact. Ultimately, people will always do exactly what they wish to do regardless of what a manager says or does and people are very good at reframing and repositioning a post hoc rationalisation and pretending to comply. Sociology texts are full of examples of this. The challenge for a coaching manager is to enable people to do just as they want for the benefit of themselves, the team and the organisation. For me this is the way forward, but I suspect there are an awful lot of people who would disagree with me on this!

Another discourse in both mentoring and coaching is the learning discourse (see Chapters 4 and 5). Often, the language of these discourses will vary in different contexts. For example, in the coaching discourse, learning and development is often linked to performance improvement but this is not so much the case in the mentoring literature where learning and development is linked, in some cases, to career progression (particularly in the USA) or elements of psychosocial development. This may also link with assumptions that the provider of the mentoring or coaching service makes about their particular context. I shall come back to this in Chapter 4. To return to contexts, Rogers (1961: 281) talks of core conditions of learning and these include: empathy, genuineness, unconditional, positive regard, and an ability to communicate all of these to others. Rogers also argues that these 'conditions' need to be in place over time for learning to develop. These become challenged when either the mentoring or coaching is conditional. Mentoring or coaching with ulterior motives is morally dubious. Wood (1970), in commenting on Kantian moral philosophy, suggests that people must be treated as 'ends in themselves' rather than 'means to an end' for the activity to be morally robust. Mentoring and coaching that is about political power and status views the mentee or coachee as a means to an end and therefore morally wrong.

Another discourse in coaching and mentoring is about transformation and change. Associated with this is a major dominant management discourse on change. We all live with slogans like *'change, change, or be changed', 'change is the only constant'* in the modern organisation. This discourse extends throughout organisational life and is influenced by technological innovation, competitive pressures and political initiatives. How far this is yet another form of managerial control and power plays is debatable but there is no doubt that the 'change agenda' has implications for people in organisations of all types and in all sectors. The consequences can be found in organisational strategies, policies for recruitment and selection, learning and development activities and health and safety (see Chapter 4). Coaches and mentors would argue that their skills and processes can help their clients to reframe their thinking, think new thoughts, and adapt to or even embrace change. Notwithstanding that therapists claim this as well, I have experienced this myself several times either as a coach/mentor or as a coachee/mentee so I would support this position, but what are the processes and skills that can help to bring these things about and are we obsessed with them?

I shall address this question in the next chapter.

4

Are We Obsessed with Skills and Competences in C&M?

introduction

As presented in Chapter 1, coaching and mentoring theory is also drawn from other frameworks in sport, developmental psychology, psychotherapy, sociology and philosophy. An ongoing debate within the coaching and mentoring worlds also links to learning and development theories. The HR profession seems to have adopted these theories in organisational contexts and this has led to an approach which inevitably involves the rational pragmatic use of skills training, competency frameworks, standards and the call for increased professionalisation not only for coaches but also mentors. This chapter takes a critical look at the question of skills and competencies in coaching and mentoring and argues for a return to the concept of the 'professional' rather than the professionally qualified or professionalisation.

The chapter first presents some propositions about learning and then links these to various dominant discourses in the organisational context. It then brings together these positions into a discussion about professionalisation versus the concept of the professional.

learning and development, coaching and mentoring

If we link coaching and mentoring to learning and development frameworks, it is first necessary to understand some key features of human learning. I would propose these cover the following:

Learning is:

- Social
- Cultural
- Situated
- Transforming
- Continuous
- A natural human experience
- Linked to moral issues.

social

Learning is a social activity (see Argyris & Schon, 1981; Boisot et al., 1996; Nonaka 1991; Polanyi, 1958) and it takes place through an interaction with other people: it is either helped or hindered by the framework of social relationships within which it occurs.

cultural

Learning is simultaneously a social and cultural activity made possible by human beings' ability to communicate with one another through a common language. Language enables us to codify our experience into bodies of knowledge and we pass this on from one generation to another. It gives us the ability to build up ideas and to confer a meaning, significance and purpose onto what we do. Cultures are also collections of values and beliefs and these influence the boundaries to learning by creating and enforcing social norms on learning. So what is acceptable for questions and challenges in one culture may not be so in another. Further, what determines an appropriate approach to learning varies from culture to culture.

situated

Learning is also a situated activity. What people learn, the pace at which they do so, the quality and depth of their understanding are very much related to the circumstances in which they live and work. People may also learn what not to do as well as what to do.

transforming

All learning involves personal transformation as new possibilities open up with further understanding. Through learning, people transform their sense of who they are and the possibilities in their lives. It provides them with a deeply personal measure of how they themselves have changed. New learning inevitably opens up new questions about the world and new possibilities in human lives. Learning generates a new sense of openness in human identities and nurtures new hopes and fears. Some organisations and settings will nurture this and some will not.

continuous

Learning takes place in all domains of human experience. It can be continuous throughout life and learning in one domain is, potentially at least, transferable to others.

natural human experience

Learning is part of human experience – hence the importance of experiential learning in contemporary management theory – but it is not only an individual experience. While it is obvious that only individuals can learn there can also be a sense of collective learning because learning is social: we learn by, with and from others and this gives a real sense in which organisations have the potential to nurture new learning.

morality

As discussed in previous chapters, within developed economies issues of manipulation, control and the abuse or uses of power are central features and within learning environments these power dynamics cannot be ignored. This is because, as Jarvis (1992: 7) puts it, '*... learning, and perhaps knowledge itself, has significant moral connotations*'. Jarvis argues that the moral dimension is inescapable in learning and knowledge acquisition. He traces his argument to the myth of Adam and Eve. Before eating from the tree of knowledge both were innocent, but afterwards they had acquired the knowledge of good and evil. Some theologians describe this event as 'the Fall' but '*Archbishop William Temple once commented that if this was a fall, it was a fall upwards! Perhaps this is the greatest paradox of all human learning – the fact that something generally regarded as good has been intimately associated with a myth of the origin evil in the world ... learning, and perhaps knowledge itself, has significant moral connotations*' (Jarvis, 1992: 7).

implications of the learning propositions

The implications of these propositions are profound. The dominating discourse of the pragmatic and rational manager often leads to the discourse of 'a manager's right to manage' that is found in organisations. This discourse, while reasonable in some respects, can also lead to a 'manager knows best' discourse and this could include 'one best way thinking', goal-dominated working practices and sometimes the inappropriate exercise of control and a misuse of power. Arguably, the evidence for this discourse could be seen, for example, in the recent rash of industrial disputes in the UK within British Airways and the British Airports Authority. HR departments, acting as agents for the pragmatic rational management, often take up and act on these arguments.

The above propositions can also help us to see that for too long most people working in modern economies have been prevented from developing their human potential to the full because few organisations have developed the environments to facilitate the very thing they profess to want – creative, innovative and self-motivated people. Not only have individuals within these environments missed the opportunities potentially open to them, but organizations and society have also lost the benefit of the further development of their most precious asset: their people. The implication here is that the rational pragmatic discourse of 'one best way' in management, a unitarist position, has no place in a true learning environment. Thus, the scientific method of cause and effect, which so dominates the management mindset, is seriously challenged and this raises issues for coaching and mentoring as well.

Added to this are clear resonances between mentoring and coaching and the above propositions. However, Cox (2006) points out that there is very little connection in the literature between adult learning and coaching despite the similarity between the two discourses. This is not to suggest that coaching writers don't make links to learning and development, they do quite often as is shown in Chapter 5, but there is not the detailed rigour in their discussions that you tend to find in the mentoring literature (see, for example, Brockbank & McGill (2006); Kram & Chandler (2005); Lankau & Scandura, (2002); Sullivan (1995).

Could this be because coaching is still a relatively new concept or term and is under-researched whereas mentoring is very well researched? And could it be that the coaching discourse employs the rational pragmatic mindset and focuses on performance rather than learning?

It may be because there are many people who have not made the links between coaching and mentoring and prefer to keep these separate – it is my experience that coaching writers do not draw too much on mentoring literature.

It may also be that, to date, the emphasis in coaching research has been return on investment (linking to a perceived management discourse) and has yet to develop insights into adult learning and coaching. And yet as is shown in the tables in Chapter 5, there are signs that in recent years the balance has shifted in the coaching literature as more people are expressing an interest in coaching.

It may also be because many of those involved with writing coaching books and papers seek to differentiate coaching from mentoring, with mentoring being positioned as an essentially voluntary activity conducted by relatively unskilled people.

In my hopeful, positive, and even idealistic moments, I would like to think that the core discourse of coaching and mentoring is an antidote to such thinking and as such it provides an alternative discourse to most mainstream management discourses. This may account for the huge increase in mentoring and coaching activity across all parts of developed and developing economies as people are crying out for a different way to relate at work. For me, the challenge is that so many practitioners and some academics seem to subscribe to the managerial discourse of the 'rational pragmatic' in order to get either coaching or mentoring going.

Another and perhaps alternative dominant discourse for the rational pragmatic manager within many different types of work organisation around the world is founded in the commonly presented slogan that management is about 'achieving results through people'. The implications for ethical behaviour are challenging here. In my view, there are two discourse imperatives in business – effectiveness and efficiency. Both are important and yet there is an inherent conflict between the two as Harrison and Smith (2001: 199) suggest: *'to do things effectively is not the same as to do them well'*. Effectiveness relates to the quality of an activity and efficiency links to time. Harrison and Smith (2001: 199) continue here by speculating as to *'whether one would prefer to be managed by the good manager or the effective manager, let alone the efficient one'*. These natural tensions may be resolved through flexibility, innovation and creativity but these may also require new ways of thinking and changes in the organisational narrative in such areas as power, status and control and I would acknowledge that it is very difficult for a manager to empower all this. The conflict here is similar to the tensions that naturally occur in learning and the concept of experiential learning could be of use in assisting a shift in position.

experiential learning

Kolb (1984), for example, clearly argues that learning from experience is a process and not a product or outcome. His framework, derived from Kurt Lewin, John Dewey and Jean Piaget, develops a set of 'structural dimensions' that underpin the process of experiential learning and lead to four different forms of knowledge, divergent, assimilative, convergent and accommodative. He views the process as cyclic but within the cycle are tensions. Kolb's model also offers two aspects of learning; gaining experience through action; gaining experience through reflection.

Action-based experience leads to 'apprehension' whereas reflective experience leads to 'comprehension'. He suggests that experience gained during action or testing is 'concrete experience'. Experience, gained through apprehension, may involve feelings about the 'heat' of the situation, the mood, the ambience. Having a concrete experience will include a whole range of events, some of which will be tangible and others intangible. The resultant knowledge, according to Kolb, is 'accommodative knowledge' or extended knowledge. Kolb (1984: 52) summarises how these forms fit together in a process of learning as follows:

> Learning, the creation of knowledge and meaning, occurs through active extension and grounding of ideas and experiences in the external world and through internal reflection about the attributes of these experiences and ideas.

Inherent in his model of learning are paradoxes and conflicts and it is these very tensions that create the conditions for learning. A task may be performed identically by two separate individuals but the resultant concrete experience may be completely different and just as relevant. It is also interesting to note that Kolb emphasises 'internal' reflection. The coach or mentor can help with 'external' reflection by helping the coachee or mentee to verbalise their thoughts and this is perhaps based on Weick's (1995: 18) notion of *'How can I know what I think until I see what I say?'* Although Kolb does not explore coaching or mentoring in the context of experiential learning, it is clear that coaching and mentoring can play an important part in facilitating learning through experience (see, for example, Alred & Garvey, 2010; Chapman, 2010) that can lead to transformation and change within the coachee or mentee.

As a result, rather than seeking to control, a mentoring or coaching manager may seek to facilitate understanding within a specific context and this could lead to new insights and change. It is not for the manager to specify the nature and form of these insights, it is for the coachee or mentee to do so in their own way. Some might see this as risky and may not be willing to take the chance on letting their power positions go, others may find that in doing so the performance they dream of starts to appear!

the change discourse

As raised in Chapter 3, another discourse is about constant change. This relates to the efficiency and effectiveness arguments in that change in an organizational context is nearly always viewed by managers as 'good' and leading to improved effectiveness or efficiency. It also links to organisational policies for recruitment and selection, learning and development, and health and safety. As Garvey et al. (2009: 96–97) indicate, this then leads to assumptions that people are needed in the workplace who can:

- adapt to change rapidly;
- be innovative and creative;
- be flexible;
- learn quickly and apply their knowledge to a range of situations;
- maintain good mental and physical health;
- work collaboratively.

They add in the pressure to perform and how it is important for '*employees to have strong and stable personalities*' (Kessels, 1996) and be able to '*tolerate complexity*' (Garvey & Alred, 2001). See Chapter 6 for a brief discussion on the psychological impact of these pressures on individuals.

This list of attributes of the modern employee could be found in most job specifications in almost any country in the world. One recent job specification, for example, for a role as a community Project Manager in Uganda, Africa, listed the following attributes:

- Strong leadership skills, including ability to build and motivate a team as well as willingness to deal with conflicts up front;
- Political and cultural sensitivity, including ability to adapt well to local cultures;
- Diplomatic and tactful;
- Proven ability to function well in a potentially volatile and sometimes stressful environment;
- Strong liaison and communication skills;
- Ability to resist external pressures;
- Innovative and creative thinking;
- Strong analytical and reporting skills.
  (http://unjobs.org/vacancies/1279743103672)

This is a challenging list and, arguably, these may not be developed via training or the competency frameworks so commonly promulgated by organisations! So, there is a problem here as well! Kessels (1996), from The Netherlands, argues that the skills and competency approaches to learning are becoming increasingly redundant. Many managers observe that this type of development simply does not deliver (see Broad & Newstrom, 1992; Groot, 1993). There are strong resonances in the above with the literature and practice of coaching and mentoring and previous chapters in this book. It seems to me that the support and potential for growth offered by coaching and mentoring addresses the issue of which key attributes people need for modern business very well on an individual basis. However, within the professional bodies for mentoring and coaching there seems to be a blockage in mindsets and an increasing emphasis on skills and competency development. This when set against the kinds of profile for the 'good' employee outlined above creates another paradoxical argument. An organisation wants and needs these attributes for its people and competency and skills frameworks do not deliver – but they do persist and the coaching and mentoring bodies promote competency frameworks for coaches and mentors! It seems that everyone is singing from the same hymnsheet but ignoring both the research and practical experience!

what's wrong with competencies?

In themselves nothing, but Garvey et al. (2009: 191) note *'when professionals are highly anxious ... under strong resource pressure, then the delivery of competencies can degrade'*. Barnett (1994: 73) goes further when he states *'the notion of competence is concerned with predictable behaviours in predicable situations'*.

These are serious observations that suggest that using competency frameworks to develop people for stable situations is probably acceptable, but set against the need to change arguments there is a problem. A competency approach to developing the skills and attributes outlined above is problematic because as Bolden and Gosling (2006: 148) suggest, there are five commonly cited problems with such frameworks:

1) The reductionist nature of competencies makes them inadequate to deal with the complexities of a job role (Ecclestone, 1997; Grugulis, 1998; Lester, 1994).
2) The generic nature of competencies means that they are not sensitive to specific situations, tasks or individuals (Grugulis, 2000; Loan-Clarke, 1996; Swailes & Roodhouse, 2003).
3) They represent a view of past performance rather than act as a predictor of future behaviour (Cullen, 1992; Lester, 1994).
4) They tend to exclude subtle qualities, interactions and situational factors (Bell et al., 2002).
5) They create a limited and mechanistic approach to learning (Brundrett, 2000).

Both coaching and mentoring are often employed to help develop people using competency frameworks, particularly in leadership development. Yet for me this presents a problem in practice where the coaching and mentoring literature emphasises individualism, autonomy, choice, variety, difference and complexity as core values, but the professional bodies call for regulation, control, standards and competencies. This is another paradox of meaning and practice and I would speculate that professional bodies are engaging in their perceptions of the dominant discourse of the rational pragmatic manager in order to engage with the management mindset. While it is imperative to do so, as I raised in the Introduction, the current practice seems to be more collusive than collaborative. Where is the critical debate?

Again, I do not suggest that the above is a malicious act but it is one that is influenced by the dominant discourse of which people become a part. Of course this is not exclusive to the coaching and mentoring professional bodies and would be no different to any other professional body or social grouping, but wouldn't the application of the coaching and mentoring approach that involves challenge and support surely be more appropriate here? We may be engaging in Argyris' (1992) concept of *'espoused theory and theory in use'* at this point, where he notes that what people say is not necessarily what they do.

There are management discourses that subscribe to the learning and development agenda but these are often from HRD professionals and consultants who seem to have to constantly struggle to communicate with the rational pragmatic manager who seeks rational pragmatic proof.

arguments in learning for competitiveness

In an age of science, technology and mass communications, economic life is driven by a competitive search for advantage and profit based on the exploitation of new knowledge. All sectors of the modern economy depend for their survival and growth on maintaining and developing ideas, skills and products, which increasingly require advanced scientific, technological and social scientific research. The results of such research are applied in all domains of social, economic and political life, acting as catalysts of social change. This means that learning and development and knowledge development are and always have been central features of economies. And yet, organisations still find it difficult to create the environments in which these can happen.

A possible explanation can be found in what could be seen as a mass societal construction of learning, based on substantial research by eminent scholars like Piaget, Jung, Levinson, Buhler, Neugarten, Kegan,

Gilligan and Kohlbergh. This positions learning in stages or phases. The intellectual movements of the last two hundred years have all conspired to make this staged view or linear picture of learning virtually irresistible and certainly dominant.

Darwinian ideas of evolution and Marxist laws of historical progress have become part of our everyday outlook. The implication of this view of learning is that it is possible to 'hurry people along' or give them a 'leg up the ladder'. More dangerously, it positions and divides people as having achieved or not achieved against a linear framework. It also connects with the idea that learning can be pre-specified in advance. While in some cases this might be a reasonable point of view, say with learning a specific skill or acquiring some core principle, the linear approach depends on goals, objectives, targets because success can be measured by whether or not these have been achieved. However, this only gets us to where we want to go by the straightest and most direct route – it cannot develop any awareness of the different kinds of destination available, the speed of travel or the choice of route, nor does it hold out any promise that we will be enriched by the outcome.

Curricula in schools across the world are based on this concept, as are university curricula and training functions in organisations. This concept has now become so familiar that we seldom notice the significance of it but children in schools are positioned by it and adults are graded by it and careers are enhanced or dashed by this concept. Every experienced coach and mentor knows that there are other ways of looking at learning that are often revealed in the central feature of learning conversations, reflection.

The act of reflection facilitated by a coach or mentor is central to the facilitated conversation and without it we cannot think new thoughts nor have new thoughts about old ideas, customs or practices. In theory at least, coachees and mentees are not being 'taught' anything but are being helped to revisit and find new ways into old truths or to have new insights or ideas. Here learning is non-linear. In this way coaches and mentors are, potentially, dealing with basic and apparently simple ideas, but in reality these are so complex, so deceptive in their simplicity, and yet so important, that they have to be approached again and again from different angles.

As Schulman (1993: 308–314) pointed out *'The more central a concept, principle, or skill to any discipline or interdiscipline, the more likely it is to be irregular, ambiguous, elusive, puzzling, and resistant to simple propositional exposition or explanation'*. Schulman realises that *'less is more'* and where we so readily think in terms of progress we have to appreciate the significance of a different set of terms: selectivity, depth, variation and richness are four that Schulman mentions.

Instead of a single, linear track the learner requires a *'criss-crossing of the landscape'*, the active application of multiple representations through metaphors, analogies, narratives and inventive examples. These require on the part of the learner *'constructions, iterations, and, most important, dialogues and debates'* (Schulman, 1993: 308–314). This seems to resonate strongly with the philosophy of coaching and mentoring and not with regulated competency frameworks. However, we are still left with the question of the professionalisation arguments where skills frameworks and competency frameworks dominate.

the skills and competency movement in coaching and mentoring

Professional bodies in the coaching and mentoring worlds have already developed or are developing competency frameworks and standards of practice, particularly for coaches. These issues present a challenging puzzle. The notion of 'standards' in educational settings for qualifications forms a core feature of curriculum design throughout the western world. The discourse around such qualifications emphasises competencies or pre-specified learning outcomes (a version of goals) and these also link to the linear model of learning presented above. This manifests in stages of qualification or a hierarchy of membership levels. The exponential growth in performance league tables for organisations and performance objectives for individuals provides evidence of this view (see Caulkin, 1995, 1997).

A straightforward explanation of this is found in Bernstein's (1971) work. He looks at curriculum design in two main ways – the open or the closed. In an open curriculum the learner leads the learning agenda, delivery is learner-led and dependent on the situation, and assessment is harder to achieve because this can only be done in relation to the learner's agenda (does this sound familiar from the coaching and mentoring literature?). In a closed curriculum the subject mater is pre-specified, delivery is content-based, and 'teacher'-led. Assessment is dominant and is easy to achieve because the learning is pre-specified. Competencies fit with the closed curriculum and therefore have appeal because they are easily measurable and thus fit with the rational pragmatic mindset.

Of course we do learn some things through a closed approach but for many issues in the workplace this is not the case. According to Bernstein (1971) the closed curriculum tends to require learners to be more compliant and less empowered, to demonstrate less initiative and little innovation or creativity. Whereas an open curriculum tends to require the learner to be less compliant and more empowered, to demonstrate more initiative and be more creative and innovative in approach. This is more in line with the attributes outlined in the previously quoted job specification.

Despite this competency frameworks are rarely challenged (see Garvey et al., 2009), even when key writers in the coaching world such as Whitmore (1992: 56–57), who is clearly anti-competencies – *'obsession with techniques killed the coaching'* and *'responsibility and awareness are the key, how you get there is not important'*, and Flaherty (1999: 13), who stated that *'techniques don't work!'*, are making their opinions be heard.

The pro-competency discourse has become so loud and so embedded in professional bodies, universities and other providers' minds that alternatives have become marginalised, or worse ignored and discounted, and risk is becoming extinct because of those who have the loudest voices. For me, this seems to offer huge risks. A recent evaluation of the London Deanery's Mentoring programme for Doctors and Dentists (Chadwick-Coule & Garvey, 2009) raised challenging questions: *"How much training or education is enough?" "Could the culture of training have negative affects on people in a competency based world where the opportunity to be not good enough is increased?"* These were based on a quotation from one mentoring doctor:

> ... you can't be an educational supervisor just because you have done it for 10 years, you need to train to be one, you can't assess a junior doctor just because you have done it for 20 years, you need to train to do it, you can't be a mentor unless you have trained to do it, as these specific trainings have come in, I have to say that I have experienced a profound loss of confidence, despite being quite a senior doctor, to the point where I would say the mentoring has added to that process of feeling that you're in the wrong, you're falling short, you're not good enough, that you're not up to standard, that perhaps you're not a very good supervisor, that perhaps you're not a very good coach. I am plagued by those kinds of thoughts in a way that is quite unhelpful, because of the development in postgraduate medical training and the kind of professionalisation of some of these roles. (Mentor)

If this is what we are doing I am very concerned, because yet again exclusion is the result rather than inclusion.

A further point, as mentioned in Chapter 2 and according to de Haan (2008), is that the relationship matters and not the model or the techniques. De Haan is referring to the relationship between coach and coachee, however, that is not the only relationship possible here. Coachees and mentees may also have a relationship with the concept of coaching or mentoring. The literature mainly emphasises the coach's or the mentor's skills and experience, but what of the notion of the skilled coachee or mentee? If both parties to the coaching or mentoring subscribe to the concept of coaching or mentoring and submit themselves to the process, there is the potential to reduce the power distance between them and thus provide an opportunity for a more balanced and productive conversation. The alternative is that the coach or mentor maintains the power position – and this may suit professional bodies and many coaches and mentors!

Professional bodies have also developed the idea of 'flying hours'. Like a pilot, a coach or mentor needs to have time to practise, reflect and experiment in order to become skilled. While in principle this seems like a good idea and it is rooted on the idea of ancient craft guilds and apprenticeships, there are also problems here. In their defence, professional bodies do ask for evidence of hours, but in my view it is the underpinning assumptions that are the difficulty and these seem, yet again, to be an attempt to quantify a human experience. Certainly hours can be counted but hours in themselves are only an indicator of development. They say nothing about the variety of experience, the quality of the experience or the coach or mentor's ability to reflect and learn from the experience. Reporting hours is simply not the same as demonstrating competence. It is a bit like someone saying that they have thirty years' experience but actually it is the same experience for thirty years! Hours reporting alone seems like a blunt instrument.

Professional bodies do however recognise the importance of continuous professional development. As raised in the Introduction, if a coach or a mentor ever thinks that they know it all it is time for them to stop! Therefore professional bodies provide, through CPD events, conferences, journals and newsletters support for continuous learning and challenge. Moreover, some engage with or commission research. This can only be a good thing. However, what does professionalisation mean?

professionalisation or professional?

Professionalisation is essentially a social norming process in which a trade or occupation sets the rules, standards and qualifications and involves compliance measures and sanctions. Professionalisation usually involves the creation of a professional body that has the function of controlling, vetting and objectifying the trade or occupation by differentiating itself as a body with integrity and competence. A professional body also defines those who are amateurs, unqualified, or of lower standing. In this way, the concept of professionalisation could be viewed either positively as creating standards of membership and practice or negatively as a narrow elitists group that excludes. Both positions are power plays.

The Dublin Declaration group called for something slightly different in that they wanted standards and codes of conduct but they also aspired to acknowledge diversity and were therefore more inclusive than exclusive in intent. The following key word extracts illustrate this:

> Establish a common understanding ... shared core code of ethics, standards of practice, and educational guidelines that ensure the quality and integrity of the competencies – acknowledge and affirm the multidisciplinary roots and nature of coaching. (Mooney, 2008: 5)

The very well-known American academic, Warren Bennis, referring to coaching, said in Morris and Tarpley (2000) *'I'm concerned about unlicensed people doing this'*. This article was probably the first to raise concerns about standards in coaching practice and Bennis used the term 'wild west of coaching' to describe what was happening back then. This term seems to have gathered momentum within the coaching world on both sides of the Atlantic and in the *Harvard Business Review* article by Stratford Sherman and Alyssa Freas called 'The Wild West of Executive Coaching' and published in 2004, this description was given more weight and obvious air time. In my view this led to a 'wild west of coaching' discourse being promoted by some professional bodies, possibly to strengthen their claim on a need for their existence or possibly to set themselves above the wild west in order to be attractive and civilised!

If we take the mentoring world, we can see a different picture. In Chapter 3 I discussed the rapid growth of social mentoring schemes to address social problems in the UK. In the USA, Garmezy (1982) pointed out that mentoring was employed on the basis of ideological or political reasons and Freedman (1999: 21) observed that that mentoring was often an *'heroic conception of social policy'* and the scramble to establish mentoring programmes for disaffected youth was *'fevor without infra-structure'*. Helen Colley, in her excellent studies in the UK, had similar findings.

It is also noteworthy that some studies, particularly US ones, (Hurley & Fagenson-Eland, 1996; Ragins & Cotton, 1996; Ragins & Scandura, 1994) show that there are potential problems with mentoring in an organisational context (see Chapter 3). For example, mentoring can be exclusive and divisive; it can encourage conformity among those with power, it can maintain the status quo and reproduce exploitative hierarchical structures (Carden, 1990; Ragins, 1989, 1994; Ragins and Cotton, 1991).

Set against this, there is also plenty of research to show that overall mentoring does work well under certain conditions (see, for example, Davies, 1999; Garvey & Garrett-Harris, 2005; Kanai & Hirakimoto, 1996; Levin-Epstein, 2003; Megginson et al., 2005; Rix & Gold, 2000).

However, the calls for professionalisation in the mentoring world are not very loud. Instead, in the UK, the European Mentoring Centre was established to become a centre of excellence rather than a professional body. The National Mentoring Network was established to support mentoring activity (this later became the Mentoring and Befriending Foundation) and in the USA the Big Brothers and Big Sisters scheme was established. None of these organisations aspired to become like professional bodies, they were more intent on supporting mentoring activity, researching it, and encouraging it to flourish. They often provide training for participants and this usually takes the form of either skills training in listening, questioning and the use of a process framework or an orientation exercise towards the design features of a particular scheme. This may be because of a strong discourse in mentoring that it is a force for good, it is generally voluntary, anyone can do it, it is unpaid and, arguably, altruistic in nature. It may also be that mentoring carries with it the credibility created by clear and strong historical roots.

Clearly this is not the whole story, but good quality research shows that mentoring is both potentially positive and negative and it persists almost as if people are prepared to tolerate the 'messiness' in the 'swampy lowlands' (see Chapter 2). Mentoring is not immune from factionalism and positioning. Helen Colley (see Chapter 3) was heckled at a conference of social mentoring scheme coordinators following the publication of her book and one well-known coach called me *'a self-centred nuisance'* when I challenged ideas put out by members of a professional body.

a possible way forward?

At the heart of coaching and mentoring activity lie trust, reflection, listening, support and challenge. These are the key attributes that seem to facilitate growth, change, learning and transformation. These are also the concepts that unite people who engage in coaching and mentoring. Of course there are many others, but progress does not mean compromising on what is agreed – the vision must remain the same but the tactics may change! The vision articulated by the Dublin Declaration states that they recognise difference but seek common ground; however, as was pointed out in previous chapters, this often articulated using the discourses of management and their associated assumptions.

One way forward is to substitute 'professionalise' with the concept of 'the professional'. In calling for 'professionalisation', there is an assumption that coaches and mentors are not professional now! This is then reinforced by 'wild west' arguments.

A professional is a member of a vocation with the vocation allied to specialised education. As argued above, competency frameworks and standards carry with them assumptions of control, simplification, reductionism, predictability and compliance. In my view this is not specialised education, rather it is pre-specified education where there are known answers. This is an important issue for several reasons. The philosopher Bertrand Russell said *'The trouble with the world is that the stupid are cocksure and the intelligent are full of doubt'*. And, *'Everything is vague to a degree you do not realize till you have tried to make it precise'*.

Competency frameworks rarely offer 'doubt' and often create a sense of precision. This results in the problem presented in the Introduction that it is possible to have 'done' coaching and mentoring! We reach the destination, but then what? Learning requires a synthesis of knowledge which results in situational decision making rather than the operation of routines or procedures. A professional must also develop new insights and understanding in the light of experience and may require further education. A professional needs to be critically reflective and reflexive about his or her own learning. This supports the idea I raised in the Introduction that we can never have 'done' coaching and mentoring because it is an ongoing journey.

For me, there is a mindset challenge here. Given the discourse in coaching and mentoring around thinking new thoughts, reframing and no predetermined answers, it seems curious that the appetite for competency frameworks and educational controls is so strong.

The previously discussed discourse of the rational, pragmatic manager is the challenge. Much of it is based on three philosophies:

- Power and control over the many by the few (articulated as the manager's right to manage).
- Newtonian concepts of cause and effect methodologies for improving efficiency and effectiveness.
- Tayloristic 'one best way' thinking.

Garvey and Williamson (2002: 194) following the attack on the World Trade Centre in New York stated:

> the old frameworks for thinking about the global order of our lives, its political fracture lines, religious and ideological diversity and its sustainability in environmental terms, are all shown to be inadequate.

Clearly, 9/11 was a horrific act. But the events which followed did not represent a change of mindsets but rather an aggressive restating of old approaches based on the lack of understanding of difference and 'west is best' thinking. I can only conclude that the arguably natural human instinct of the 'intolerance' (see Back, 2004; Bhavnani et al., 2005) of difference seems to be a major challenge right across all sectors of global society.

There are two issues here. The first is that 'intolerance' does not imply that the opposite concept – 'tolerance' – is any less problematic. What a dominant group may see as normal, a minority group may see as an aberration worthy of punishment or vice versa. Some may see the concept of 'toleration' as an acceptance or 'putting up with' an unacceptable custom or behaviour. Such a position could be viewed as moral relativism and as such it would have dubious connotations. It is also difficult to separate tolerance from power. A dominant group may have more of a choice to 'tolerate' than a minority group would. The minority may simply have to 'endure', 'suffer in silence' or 'put up with' a dominant group's perspective.

Alred and Garvey (2010: 526) suggest that 'tolerance' has at least two meanings.

> One is about '… putting up with'. Tolerance in this sense implies that a person views situations as, simplistically tolerable or intolerable so that the very perception of a situation becomes part of what makes it more or less tolerable. This, we believe, chips away at the personal qualities and abilities that determine optimal performance.

The second meaning they put forward (2001: 256) is:

> … closer to its etymological root [and means] 'to sustain', to keep going and remain effective in prevailing conditions.

The second quote offers a more positive perspective and involves aspects of the Rogerian concept of 'positive regard' for difference raised in Chapter 3. An alternative to 'positive regard' may be found in the concepts of 'civility' or 'pluralism'. These ideas include the notion of 'acceptance'.

The second issue is that 'instinct' is not underpinned with knowledge and therefore there is no understanding or insight for an 'instinct'. For all people, this is a very serious issue – probably the most serious we face – but it is also deeply problematic. 'Acceptance' or 'tolerance' or any other concept in the context of diversity is a blend of the rational and the emotive. Many organisations attempt to 'manage' diversity and lever it for strategic or social benefit and this is a completely rational choice – it makes sense. However, making sense of anything is a construction based on individual and societal narratives. People have within them a narrative line about themselves and about others. These narratives influence behaviours and by exploring an individual's narrative and seeking alternative positions, understanding, tolerance and acceptance become possible. This is the challenge of Position 3 thinking, which is outlined in Chapter 3.

In diversity there are no easy ways forward, but in the context of learning and development diversity is an essential characteristic of the creative process. It is not about 'putting up' with each other but more about creating a genuine tolerance, acceptance and understanding of difference, living with it as normal rather than defining others by their differences and as outsiders. Bruner's (1990) view is that meaning is distributed through dialogue and here is the link to mentoring and coaching. A mentoring and coaching dialogue offers the potential to explore dominate narratives and meanings, develop understanding and explore the emotive as well as the rational – and this takes place with Position 3 thinking!

Professional bodies have a key leadership role to perform in all this. Leadership, in my opinion, is more about the toleration and acceptance of difference than an imposition of controls and the expectation of compliance. For me leadership is about helping people to come together, to be inspired and to resolve differences. Leadership based on compliance is morally dubious, fails to recognise individuality and difference, and stifles creativity and the human spirit. The Ancient Greek philosopher Aristotle was supposed to have said '*It is the mark of an educated mind to be able to entertain a thought without accepting it*'. In my view, this is the central challenge of diversity.

Perhaps it is time to stop all the jostling for position and start getting the message out using the discourse of coaching and mentoring rather than adopting other people's discourses, thus confusing the marketplace and diluting the message. One such discourse is that of performance. This is discussed in the next chapter.

5

What is Performance in Coaching and Mentoring?

Within the management setting, there is a strong discourse about performance in general. As raised in previous chapters, an espoused central purpose for coaching and mentoring activity is improved performance. However, performance can be construed in many different ways. This chapter takes these discourses and critically discusses them. It then offers an alternative perspective as a way forward.

introduction

Within the coaching literature the general thrust is about improved performance over a short timescale, but different authors have a different emphasis on performance and interpret the concept differently. In some ways, as this chapter will show, the discourse of performance within coaching attempts to tap into the managerial discourse of the fast moving, ever changing, focused, performance-oriented manager.

Within the mentoring literature performance is often positioned as developmental and holistic and viewed as a longer-term objective. This discourse taps into the altruistic, voluntary discourse of social mentors but there are signs that the US perspective of career sponsorship is developing within Europe and especially the UK.

the coaching performance discourse

As mentioned in Chapter 1 coaching has long been associated with performance improvement, from its earliest reference in history and through to its association with sport and, later on, the business world. Today there are numerous books on coaching with 'performance' in the title, suggesting that the quest for improved performance is a strong attraction to the management book-buying public.

Whitmore (2002: 97), influenced by Gallwey (1974), states that *'real performance is going beyond what is expected; it is setting one's own highest standards, invariably standards that surpass what others demand or expect'.* He stresses the importance of *'focused attention'* by the coachee as this, in his view, leads to an improved performance. Interestingly, he suggests that *'even managers who use coaching widely may fail if they focus exclusively on performance improvement'* (p. 101). He also suggests that, *'self-esteem is the lifeblood of performance at work'* (p. 114). These are curious statements made by one of the originators of the GROW model of coaching. GROW emphasises the development of the 'goal' as a starting point for performance improvement – an idea drawn from the sporting world – but these statements highlight something other than the 'goal'. For me they hint at the (sometimes unspoken) pressure imposed on the coachee by a coaching manager who is anxious to get them to surpass what is expected – a power play. Set against this is the acknowledgement that performance is strongly linked to the 'inner self' where personal senses of power or self-esteem are the real differentiators between the excellent and the mediocre. This notion resonates with the ideas presented in all the previous chapters in this book about the social contexts influencing behaviours and outcomes. In this case, performance is also a product of the environment in which it happens. Therefore managers and coaching managers can create an environment for high performance or they cannot. However, could Whitmore be suggesting that performance is also a matter of personal perception rather than something that is achieved by reference to external measures or 'goals'? This would fit with some aspects of sporting analogies where concepts like *'personal best performance'* (see, for example, Elliot & Conroy, 2005) are drivers of performance. As will be discussed later in this chapter, this 'personal best' concept is also problematic. Whitmore was a successful sportsman in his life and this may help explain his position. However, the emphasis on goals in Whitmore's model remains a curious paradox and one that is very open to multiple interpretations.

Wilson (2007: 8) follows the Whitmore line but she tends towards a strongly 'internal' or personal view of performance when she states that coaches *'enable coachees to develop their knowledge about themselves and thereby improve performance in their personal and their working lives'.*

Downey (2003: 15), also strongly influenced by Gallwey (1974), defines coaching as *'the art of facilitating the performance, learning and development of others'.* He tends to downplay the significance of learning and development in coaching by suggesting that this is what sustains the improvement, but that removing the sources of interference that impede (as indicated by Gallwey) performance through a non-directive approach to questioning is central to coaching. Taking a slightly different position to Whitmore, Downey emphasises the development of Performance Goals, Learning Goals and Success Measures at the start of coaching relationships. Interestingly, Downey also refers to coachees as 'players' and this may indicate a sporting influence in his thinking.

Parsloe and Wray (2000: 12) suggest that coaching is *'typically result or performance oriented with the emphasis on taking action'* and Berglas (2002: 5) comments that coaching offers *'the promise of quick and painless improvement of performance'* and is often applied when there is a problem with performance. The 'quick' element seems to resonate with the notion of short-term improvement, a discourse very much in favour with the manager looking for quick results. With reference to timescales in performance being so often used to differentiate mentoring from coaching, Flaherty (2005: 23) adopts an interesting position by stating that the results of coaching are linked to long-term excellent performance, self-correction, and self-generation. He suggests that coaching *'allows for people to change, to become more competent, and to become excellent at performance'*. This is particularly interesting because it is mentoring that is most often positioned as having a long-term effect rather than coaching. Flaherty is perhaps repositioning coaching away from the short-term in order to link to the sustainability arguments used in management.

The Association of Coaching report of 2004 supports the strong discourse of performance in coaching. It states that the main reason for seeking executive coaching is to improve performance. However, when examined there are many other factors that contribute to performance in the report but it does provide an interesting general pointer as to an executive preoccupation – performance! Thus, in emphasising performance improvement in the Association of Coaching report the authors are linking this directly to the management discourse.

A further indication as to the dominant discourses in coaching literature can be seen in Figure 5.1 below. Using EBSChost, a business publications database, I first searched only peer reviewed publications with the word 'coaching' in the title with the words 'performance' or 'goals' published between 1983 and 2000 and then 2000–2010. I then substituted the words 'learning' or 'development' and searched between the same dates. After that I repeated the exercise for all publications in the database between the same dates.

The chart shows that 'gold standard' researchers had little interest in researching coaching and performance linked to goals between 1983 and 2000. Between 2000 and 2010 this increased slightly. For learning and development research in coaching there is a different pattern. Between 1983 and 2000, there were many more research-based publications and this almost doubled in number between 2000 and 2010.

There is a curious change in the pattern for 'All' publications finding. Before 1983, there were very few articles about coaching and performance

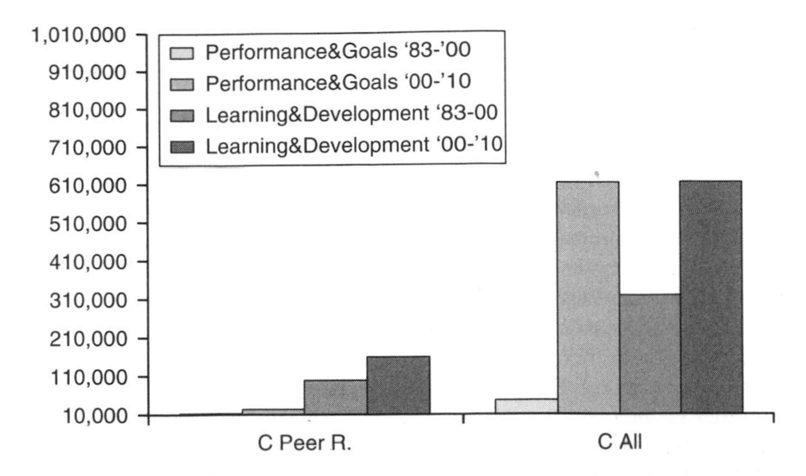

Figure 5.1 Themed articles on coaching

linked to goals but between 2000 and 2010 there was a massive increase. However, between 1983 and 2000, there were many more publications on coaching and learning and development than for the same period for performance and goals: this almost doubles between 2000 and 2010 to reach the same number of publications as there were for performance and goals in the same period.

The year 2000 also showed the first hint of 'wild west of coaching' appearing in the discourse and perhaps this influenced the shift in focus. It is interesting that the literature I have quoted throughout this book is generally thought of as high quality and bestselling work, but it tends, to focus on the performance elements more than the learning and development and this is clearly in opposition to the publication pattern in this database. One argument is that performance is a product of learning and so perhaps there is not quite the discrepancy as would first appear. However, these links between performance and learning and development are rarely made explicit in the context of coaching (Cox, 2006). The huge increase in publications in general on matters related to coaching over the period 2000–2010 is also noteworthy. This suggests considerable social interest in coaching activity.

There are numerous texts on the concept of performance within coaching all of which tap into various versions of the discourse of performance. As discussed in *Coaching and Mentoring: Theory and Practice* by Garvey, Stokes and Megginson (2009), the current dominant mode of research is about providing 'evidence' that coaching is cost effective. This is an example of a dominant discourse in business being employed in order to develop coaching activity. However, few writers are specific about what they mean by performance – although a meta study by De Meuse and Dai (2008) identifies skills improvement, changes in job attitudes and the clarification of organisational vision and mission as commonly cited benefits in coaching research. But they also noted that coachees tended to report more improvement than others do and that when the evaluation study is aligned to the objectives for coaching, the performance improvement is large.

On one level this looks encouraging, on another – as discussed in Chapter 4 – a pre-specified objective can simply construct that which has been pre-specified and offer little in the way of alternative routes to achievement or change. In my view this is another version of the 'one best way' rational pragmatic discourse, but this time it is applied in another context. It may also suggest that pre-specification simply engineers a positive result. So are we fooling ourselves here?

In summary, there seems to be a few (but influential) voices in the coaching for performance discourse and a very widespread interest in the business context in both coaching for performance and coaching for learning and development. The discourse seems to be aimed at the manager who, it is assumed, is looking for ways to become more competitive by improving performance. This may account for the rise and rise of coaching within the business world.

the mentoring performance discourse

In a seminal work, Levinson et al. (1978: 97) position mentoring as an important contributor to development. They suggest:

> The mentor relationship is one of the most complex, and developmentally important, a man can have in early adulthood ... No word currently in use is adequate to convey the nature of the relationship we have in mind here ... The term 'mentor' is generally used in a much narrower sense, to mean teacher, adviser or sponsor. As we use the term, it means all these things, and more.

Some others (e.g. Murray &Owen, 1991: 4), quite readily take a narrower view:

> Facilitated mentoring is a structure and series of processes designed to create effective mentoring relationships, guide the desired behaviour change of those involved, and evaluate the results for the protégés, the mentor and the organization.

This rather mechanistic or perhaps pragmatic view of mentoring positions mentoring as a 'tool' or a 'lever' to achieve performance enhancement in individuals.

In her early work in the USA, Kram (1985) suggested that mentoring performed two main functions under the banner of her term 'psychosocial function'. One is a 'career' function where the mentee would learn appropriate skills and knowledge in order to perform the job function. This would include preparing for a career progression (including sponsorship), developing further opportunities to learn, offering exposure to higher and different levels in the career structure and support. The other is helping to develop competence, confidence and clarity about their identity in the context of work and about the meaning of professional effectiveness. This also includes role modelling, counselling support and perhaps friendship. Kram's seminal work is very widely cited. This book, in my view, was the antecedent of a dominant discourse of mentoring. However, there have been some assumptions built from this foundation.

Firstly, mentoring scheme management guides often promise improved performance (for example, Murray & Owen, 1991, and Wilson & Elman, 1990) and this performance improvement is often linked to career advancement. Indeed, many people see career advancement as a measurable performance benefit of mentoring activity. However, performance alone is not necessarily a prerequisite to career advancement. Power, relationship networks and organisational politics all play an important role in career progression (Kirchmeyer, 2005) and perhaps this is a strong argument for mentoring activity in that it does seem to show Kram's eclectic concept of the 'psychosocial function'. It has to be borne in mind, however, that as was discussed in Chapter 1 this is the US model for mentoring. However, what emerges for me is that the mentoring discourse seems to be appealing to individuals rather than managers and that organisations are more relaxed about mentoring than they are about coaching. Many organisations who adopt mentoring may view it as a gesture for the individual to maintain interest and motivation. In a meta-study by Garvey and Garrett-Harris (2005) they show that mentoring is also associated with staff retention.

Emmerik (2008), in a study in The Netherlands, suggests that it is not just mentoring that helps improve performance but also the combined influences of both individual and team support. This research provides additional evidence for the idea that learning is a social activity and points to the notion raised in Chapter 4 that learning and performance are social practices and not necessarily solo activities.

Garvey and Garrett-Harris (2005) noted that 63 per cent of the citations in over 100 published articles on the benefits of mentoring were linked directly to motivation and performance improvement. They also noted that 'performance' could be widely defined as including, *'business*

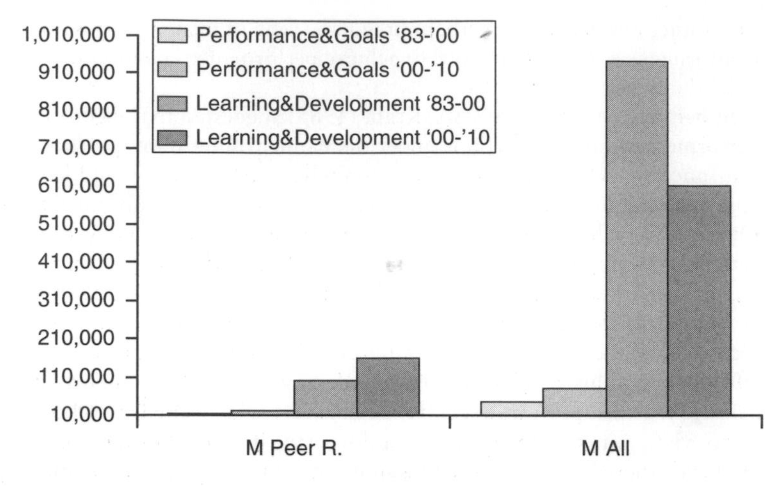

Figure 5.2 Themed articles on mentoring

performance, reduced re-offending rates or improved behaviour in School, and effective implementation of policies' (p. 11).

Mentoring activity, like coaching, is also linked to performance improvement. However, the discourse is perhaps slightly different. To illustrate this, I repeated the exercise described above in the previous section on coaching for the mentoring literature: some interesting results are set out in Figure 5.2. Here, the peer-reviewed searches show that the dominant preoccupation for mentoring researchers appears to be learning and development. This increased between 2000 and 2010, whereas performance and goals research publications remained quite low in comparison to learning and development.

When looking at the 'All' publications category, between 1983 and 2000 there were vast numbers of articles on learning and development and mentoring: this declined between 2000 and 2010. In looking at the performance and goals literature for these periods these remained fairly low. The simple searches seem to highlight that learning and development are key themes in the mentoring discourse but that this declined in the period 2000 to 2010.

Figure 5.3 shows a comparison between publications in the area of coaching and mentoring. The decrease in publications in the areas of learning and development in mentoring between 2000 and 2010 coincided with the increase in coaching publications in learning and development during the same period. This perhaps reflected a shift in the discourses in both mentoring and coaching in those ten years. It is interesting to note that the 'learning organisation' literature first appeared in the 1990s and during this period interest in

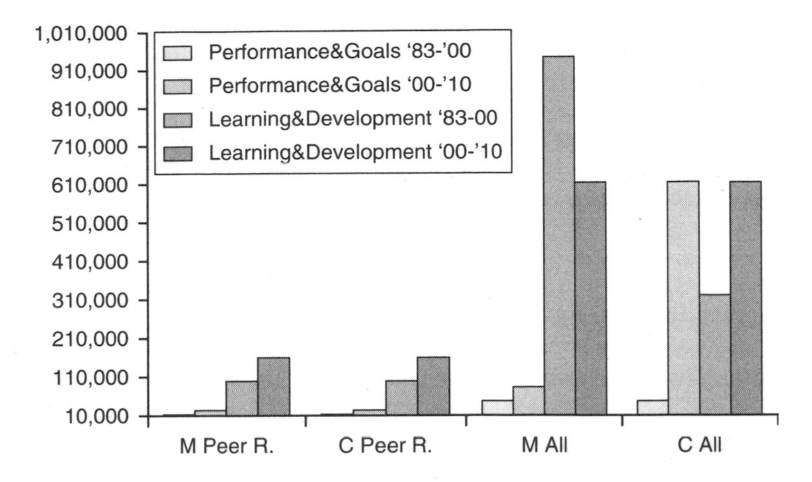

Figure 5.3 Themed articles on mentoring and coaching

the learning route to business performance and sustainable growth developed and grew. Senge's book, *The Fifth Discipline*, published in 1990, was reviewed in 1997 in the *Harvard Business Review* as one of the seminal works of the previous seventy-five years. Arguably mentoring and later coaching discourses were linked to the learning and development discourse of this period.

the managerial performance discourse

Performance is a preoccupation for many mangers and leaders in an organisational context. The world of management literature is littered with publications of all type on the subject of performance. In essence, there seem to be three main discourses in all of this literature:

- Performance by Measurement
- Performance through Development
- A combination of the two.

Linked to these discourses are other discourses, for example performance:

- Through reward
- Leadership or management style
- Through learning and development
- Concepts of power and control.

The measurement discourse lies at the heart of the rational pragmatic discourse and gives rise to commonly professed slogans like:

- 'If you can't measure it, you can't manage it'.

Or interestingly, in this era of large bonuses and severance packages for executives,

- 'if you don't measure results, you can't tell success from failure and thus you can't claim or reward success or avoid unintentionally rewarding failure'.

Or quite worryingly,

- 'What gets measured, gets done'.

In an interesting book, *Trust in Numbers: The Pursuit of Objectivity in Science and Public Life,* Porter (1995: 45) states '*Numbers create and can be compared with norms, which are among the gentlest and yet most pervasive forms of power in modern democracies*'. He goes on to suggest that the links between objectivity and numbers become significant in social contexts where trust is lacking, leadership is weak, and private negotiation is morally suspect. This challenging statement is particularly significant in a performance by measurement environment. In other words, measurement becomes the fall back position for poor leadership and management!

Worse, Amabile (1997) shows that strict, controlling, measurement-driven management inhibits innovation and creativity and is a form of social coercion as people are ranked, included or excluded, and differentiated. An alternative interpretation on the positive side is that performance measurements for those that meet the standard can make them feel valued, unique, and perhaps indispensable. Whatever the case, learning and development activities will be challenged in these environments unless the learner internalises the discourse of the organisation or at least 'buys into it'. If there are substantial financial rewards I think this is more likely! However, both positions will lack coherence in an environment in which coaching and/or mentoring are vehicles for performance and development and the dominant discourse of C&M is supposed to be about the learner's agenda.

In the measurement and controlling environment, it is important to raise questions about who will decide on what is measured and who will decide on who is responsible for an individual's learning and performance?

If the answers to these questions are, 'the manager' both the model and the discourse will simply break down. And yet this remains the discourse in many organisations in developed and developing economies alike.

Winstanley and Stuart-Smith's (1996: 66) comments are that *'traditional models and approaches to performance management generally do not succeed in meeting their objectives, are flawed in implementation, act to demotivate staff, and are often perceived as forms of control which are inappropriately used to "police" performance'*. They go on to suggest that this is not just a question of performance but also one of ethics in management. They apply a Kantian philosophy where treating people as a 'means to an end' rather than an 'end in themselves' is fundamentally immoral. The espoused discourse within coaching and mentoring of 'the learner's agenda' is, in essence, a humanistic and moral position which links to Kantian philosophy. However, Winstanley and Stuart-Smith (1996) suggest that in a performance-managed environment people will generally feel that they are simply a 'means to an end'.

It seems to me that yet again the central issue of 'power' is, in organizational contexts, assumed to be the manager's and attributed to them. This always has the potential to prove problematic.

alternative discourses

The above discussion is a complex one and finding a way through it is challenging. The subject of 'performance' is clearly central to management thinking and has a strong place in the arguments for both coaching and mentoring. The desire for outcomes, a target driven performance and measurement systems that demonstrate performance is linked to the discourses found in sport. Given that the business world is dominated by men and, in my experience, men are attracted to sport, the extension of sporting ideas on motivation and performance has become attractive (Stelter, 2009). This is strengthened by the fact that many successful sporting people will make a living by translating sporting ideas into a business context. As raised in Chapter 3, when I worked in consultancy, we used to run a roadshow led by famous ex-sports people. These were well attended and I always felt, not surprisingly really, that the famous sportsperson was the attraction rather than the content of what we did! While sport is about motivation, performance and competition, in my view it does not reflect the complexity of the business world – but managers are persuaded by the analogies and the obvious simplicity of sporting arguments that at best are about faster, longer, higher, more, and winning and losing. Also, sporting performance is often more short term than that of business cycles.

Coaching and mentoring activity flourishes when there is a recognition of the subtle and complex ways in which individual performance and fulfilment can be enhanced by one-to-one discussions and when support is provided in appropriate ways throughout the organisation (Kirchmeyer, 2005). For me, the areas that seem to give most cause for concern in business life will be rooted in an individual's personal qualities – the attributes for practical judgements. This is because skill and knowledge acquisition is relatively easy to achieve (it is certainly more easily measured) through the rational approach but the personal attributes associated with social interaction are not. These attributes do have a major impact on an individual's ability to learn and apply knowledge and skills. They also represent the values that drive human behaviour. The literature on coaching and mentoring is full of personal attributes, emotional stability, behaviour change arguments and the link that can be made to coaching or mentoring activity as facilitating the acquisition of these attributes.

If a 'target' or 'goal' approach is applied to coaching and mentoring (as is often the case) it may not yield the desired outcome of enhanced individual learning. This is because the espoused positions for coaching and mentoring are more about developing the whole person than developing specific skills or knowledge. An organisation that engages in 'whole person' development using a technical and rational approach is therefore likely to be disappointed with the outcome.

The dominant discourses found in coaching and mentoring suggest to me that these are perhaps early signs of a shift in view from *'if you can't measure it, you can't manage it'* towards a more qualitative approach that recognises that there is more to human performance at work than simple measurement. This of course may be sheer optimism on my part! However, if this is the case it is crucial that the learning and development-driven approach to strategic advantage recognises the need to develop managers who can create the appropriate learning environments to support learning and encourage autonomy at the same time as committing to the organisational purpose, will who are able to genuinely listen and moderate their controlling instincts.

Other environments where performance is important will have different ways of supporting their people – for example, the performing arts. In a musical performance the nature of a particular performance is complex: there are rules set by the score, the performance notes, the instruments, and the limits of the performers; but the music, collectively played, is unique to that performance, to that occasion. A good conductor is someone who knows they cannot control everything that happens but rather will allow the fullest participation of each player within the vision and spirit of the music. The classical recording industry thrives on the variety of performance that arises from the complexity of performing groups of musicians. What is new in a performance, the emergent innovation, is heard most explicitly when musicians improvise and it is striking that Drucker (1992) and Barrett (1998) have used the improvising jazz band as a metaphor for learning at work. The point made here reminds us again of the importance of informal learning, of learning that departs from the rules, that moves away from overt training and instruction, and appears within the daily flow and flux of experience at work. This is the province of coaching and mentoring.

My colleague, David Megginson, in some focus group studies with experienced coaches, has raised the question of *'whether a performance coach should focus on performance'*. He identified three main overlapping discourses:

- Performance management
- Performance coaching
- Developmental coaching.

It would seem the way forward here is to conceive of performance within coaching and mentoring as an eclectic mix that may contribute to a performance management system as well as being developmental. The concept here is that performance is primarily a function of learning and development activity rather than a measurement system.

Within the coaching and mentoring worlds no one discourse, in my view, is stronger than any other at the present time, but over time dominant ones will emerge probably as professional bodies become stronger and more powerful. But when it comes to thinking critically about coaching or mentoring it is important to try to ask *'which discourse is the speaker or writer connecting to?'* The answers may be many, but for me it is also important to remember that a number is just a number and it is humans that attach meaning to it just as humans attach meaning to language – and neither of these holds the monopoly on universal truth!

6

The Psychological Influences on Coaching and Mentoring

In this book so far the issue of discourse has been a regular theme. There are many discourses in coaching and mentoring and one which deserves a chapter in its own right is the psychological debate.

As outlined in previous chapters, many people lay claims to coaching and this seems to be allied to the human need for control. In my view this yet again raises questions about the motivations of those who seek to claim (mainly) coaching and (to a lesser extent) mentoring as their own. This chapter will examine the various discourses within the psychology world.

what is the psychology of coaching discourse?

The coaching literature seems to be far more concerned with psychology than the mentoring literature does and the discourse is very different to that found in the mentoring literature. Within the coaching psychology discourse in general there is a more strident debate that is perhaps more about positioning theory than building it.

As raised in Chapter 4, there are pressures placed on people in the workplace to acquire and develop and array of personal and interpersonal skills. In a powerful article, Arnaud (2003) makes a link between the sporting philosophies found within the business sector that are based on a competitiveness which is *'more bitter, individualistic and prevalent in the workplace now than ever before'* (p. 1132). He goes on to say that the increased pressure to perform boosts the drivers for individual employability because poor job security then promotes a need for *'personalized counselling, both on the part of those most directly concerned ... and on the part of the heads of organizations and top executives'* (p. 1132). For Arnaud, this explains the rise of coaching with a psychological dimension and these approaches range from *'post-Rogerian techniques to clinical approaches'* (p. 1132). In order to live, work and function in the modern capitalist world there are huge pressures on people that are very likely to have a psychological impact.

Many definitions and descriptions previously raised in this book place coaching in the domain of behaviouristic and humanistic psychology. Stober (2006) agrees that the philosophical foundation for coaching is within the discipline of humanistic psychology and suggests that change and human development are central concepts to its practice. A simple look at the sheer variety of models of coaching that are in the marketplace (see Garvey et al., 2009) suggests that many of the approaches to coaching – such as the person-centred approach, Gestalt, existentialism, and psychotherapy – all have their roots in this humanistic perspective. In *The Complete Handbook of Coaching* (Cox et al., 2010) of 29 chapters 14 are directly linked to various psychological and therapy based underpinnings. In fact the publishers classify the book under their psychology series. Garvey et al. (2009) suggest that these approaches or models of coaching are presented to the market as branded products.

The psychodynamic perspective largely stems from classic Freudian psychoanalysis which includes perspectives on individual experiences and unconscious mental processes. These may involve the mechanisms which impede or facilitate performance, a willingness to change and to learn. Within the coaching literature these issues tend to be presented non-pathologically or as attitudes, emotions and behaviours which create only mildly dysfunctional behaviour. These may include: dependency, defensiveness, aggression, attitudes towards authority figures and power, fight or flight, escapism, denial, passivity, sense of responsibility and commitment, assumptions, acceptance, control, security and insecurity, conflict, avoidance, confidence, anxiety and stress, projective identification, transference and counter-transference.

This illustrative list probably represents the most common issues discussed between coach and coachee in practice.

Another element of humanistic psychology is the concept and practice of positive psychology within coaching. There seems to be a closer integration of this element of psychology with coaching than other psychological ideas and the field appears to be growing. The linkage, according to Linley and Harrington (2005: 15), probably first appeared in *'Martin Seligman's 1998 Presidential Address to the American Psychological Association'* and in the UK *'The Psychologist (Linley, Joseph & Boniwell, 2003) was devoted to the topic, and the First European Positive Psychology Conference was held in Winchester in June 2002'*. Linley and Harrington suggest that there are three clear links:

1 Positive psychology is concerned with performance enhancement.
2 It focuses, as its name suggests, on the positive side of human nature and locates this within the socially constructed arena – the environment is important.
3 It is interested in the notion of 'human strength'.

In general term, positive psychology has an interest in the following areas:

- Happiness;
- The good life – self-efficacy, personal effectiveness;
- Flow – intense concentration and awareness;
- Mindfulness – focusing on the immediate experience or being in the moment;
- The meaningful life – optimism, self talk, spirituality;
- Good work;
- Strengths and virtues – wisdom and knowledge; courage; humanity; justice; temperance; transcendence.

While there is much to admire in this philosophy, there are weaknesses in this approach that are potentially harmful. Of course, positive psychologists are likely to say that positive psychology is not the same as positive thinking (mmmm – not sure about that) but the real danger here is that people may start to feel that when bad things happen to them it is their own fault because they were not thinking positively enough! Also, there may be a risk that by focusing so much on the positive an individual may not address their problems and slip into denial. These are dangerous thoughts indeed!

This is exactly the point made in *Smile or Die: How Positive Thinking Fooled America and the World*, by Barbara Ehrenreich (2009). In this we hear how the positive approach taken by the health practitioners who surrounded her following her diagnosis of breast cancer was relentless in encouraging her to embrace the disease positively because it would aid recovery. There are many other claims in scientific journals that positive thinking is helpful to the biology of people (see, for example, Bandura, 1977; Fredrickson et al., 2000).

Many advocates of positive psychology also claim a scientific basis for their approach, particularly in coaching psychology. Biswas-Diener and Dean (2007), for example, clearly state that positive psychology is a science and support this with the comment that the research on the topic is published in *'high quality academic journals'* (p. viii). There is no doubt that there is a large body of 'evidence' which suggests that there may be something in this, but as a biochemist herself Ehrenreich states:

> My response when confronted with the 'positive attitude will help you battle and survive this experience' brigade was to rail against the use of militaristic vocabulary and ask how miserable the optimism of the 'survivor' would make the poor woman who was dying from her breast cancer. It seemed to me that an 'invasion' of cancer cells was a pure lottery. No one knows the cause. (Murray, 2010)

She goes on to suggest that America in general suffers from the delusion that *'all is for the best in the best possible worlds'* and this is potentially damaging. This is perhaps similar to the experienced doctor in Chapter 4 who felt inadequate when faced with more training. The best of intentions can be interpreted in several ways and positive psychology is not without its critics. So where does that leave the free choice to be what one wants to be? The *'because it's good for you'* argument strikes me as patronising and too simplistic here!

Held (2004: 12) seems to support my view when she challenges what she calls the *'dominant, polarizing Message: Positivity is good and good for you; negativity is bad and bad for you'*. She suggests that there is dominant discourse within the positive psychology movement that is divisive and polarising. She adds: *'The tyranny of the positive attitude lies in its adding insult to injury: If people feel bad about life's many difficulties and they cannot manage to transcend their pain no matter how hard they try (to learn optimism), they could end up feeling even worse; they could feel guilty or defective for not having the right (positive) attitude, in addition to whatever was ailing them in the first place'*.

Ehrenreich supports this position from her lived experience and noted there was no evidence that positive thinking did improve survival rates among cancer patients. What there are, however, are improved diagnosis and detection, better surgical techniques, an improved understanding of treatments and an improved targeting of these treatments and she argues that this is what makes the difference: positive thinking simply created for her *'an additional burden to an already devastated patient'* (Murray, 2010). I can see her point! It seems to me that positive thinking is normal, but then again so is negative thinking – it is what makes us human and, as discussed in Chapter 1, 'truth' and the evidence to support 'truthfulness' are often a matter of philosophical preference.

To return to the concept of alethic pluralism first raised in Chapter 1, as a scientist Ehrenreich looked for evidence that positive thinking improved survival rates for cancer suffers. Her search for evidence seems to me to be based in both the Correspondence and Pragmatism versions of truth and these led to her rejection of the positive thinking philosophy. However, from a Coherence perspective, the arguments still did not make sense to her and she also rejected the Consensus position as *'mass delusion'*. My comment above that there is plenty of evidence links with the supporters of positive coaching psychology in a Consensus view of truth – so I'm at it as well!

On the plus side she states that she does not *'write in a spirit of sourness or personal disappointment, nor do I have any romantic attachment to suffering as a source of insight or virtue. On the contrary, I would like to see more smiles, more laughter, more hugs, more happiness ... and the first step is to recover from the mass delusion that is positive thinking'* (Murray, 2010). Perhaps in my language Position 3 thinking (see Chapter 3) offers a way forward.

Another discourse found in Grant's (2007) work is the question of whether coaching is merely a more socially acceptable form of therapy. This seems particularly important in an organisational context in which competitive pressure can create an environment where the confession of any form of psychological or internal conflict may be perceived as a weakness. Grant and Palmer (2002: 2), two big and well-respected names in coaching psychology, offer *'coaching psychology is for enhancing performance in work and personal life domains with normal, non-clinical populations, underpinned by models of coaching grounded in established therapeutic approaches'*.

Grant and Palmer are clearly unequivocal about the therapeutic grounding necessary for the coaching psychologist. Like other disciplines psychology has many branches, and to be fair they do not seem to make any judgement in this definitional statement that without a grounding in therapy coaching does not exist – they seem particularly careful to use the term *'coaching psychology'*. This adds clarity on their position that coaching psychology is one specific version.

It is also interesting that Grant and Palmer evoke the 'performance discourse' in their definition – perhaps as an attempt to match with the performance discourse which dominates management (see Chapter 5) or possibly the 'performative' dominated approach to learning and knowledge development as outlined in Chapter 1. Thus, potentially, in order to 'fit in' with a particular client base? However, it is interesting that Parsloe and Wray (2000) differentiate coaching from therapy when they assert that coaching is an action taking, results and performance-oriented process that produces and sustains change over time. This sounds like a Pragmatists' perspective aimed at appealing to the rational pragmatic manager. This view also contradicts Grant and Palmer's position and I may be naive but therapists might surely claim the same thing as Parsloe and Wray suggest? Allied to this is another discourse, articulated by Whitmore (1997), which suggests that coaching is proactive and therapy is reactive – another curious generalisation given that some therapeutic approaches (for example, cognitive behavioural therapy and rational emotive behavioural therapy) are quite proactive in approach. In addition Carroll (2003) suggests that counselling is a remedial activity, with Parsloe and Wray (2000) pointing out that therapy is grounded in extensive theory and therefore they would indicate that coaching is not about therapy. Are they saying that coaching is not grounded in theory and thus supporting Brunner's (1998: 516) position that coaching is '*a domain devoid of any fixed deontology*'?

A more plausible distinction from Grant (2001: 5) that supports Carroll (2003) suggests that coaching is essentially for a 'normal population' whereas counselling, '*regardless of differences in techniques and philosophies between psychotherapeutic schools, clinical psychotherapy per se is primarily remedial and concerned with repairing or curing dysfunctionality*'.

Thus, perhaps therapy is for the dysfunctional with a 'healing' or 'remedial' agenda and coaching psychology is for the 'worried well'! This may suit the coaching discourse which asserts very strongly that coaching is not remedial, despite it being used as such in a range of organisations (Berglas, 2002). However, Foucault (2006) argues very forcibly that mental health is a social construction and not a scientific fact! Society decides what is 'normal' and what is 'deviant' and this may vary from context to context.

There is another interesting discourse, in three parts, in the psychology of coaching world:

1 'There is not much empirical research on coaching!' (Evers et al., 2006; Grant, 2003; Kampa-Kokesch & Anderson, 2001).
2 'There are academic papers on the subject!' (Biswas-Diener & Dean, 2007; Law et al., 2007).
3 'A stronger research base is needed.' (Cox & Ledgerwood, 2003).

I do this as well I must confess. (Garvey et al., 2009) with the notion of coaching in general rather than specifically linked to coaching psychology. There is a question here about what sort of research. Psychology has traditionally endorsed positivistic research – '*most of modern psychology in the 20th century was devoted to the creation of this scientific foundation with its emphasis on mathematically testable hypotheses, reliable and valid controlled studies, clearly defined measures, and findings that can be challenged by colleagues who could repeat the reported experiments*' (Kilburg, 2004: 205).

I think herein lies a problem. Without getting into an analysis of all publications in psychological research for the last 100 years, it is clear that the results from the main body of psychological research are largely inconclusive, variable and mixed. Comparisons between various therapies and treatments have produced a zero result for the efficacy of one approach over the other (Wampold et al., 1997: 203) and yet the research continues in the same vein as research psychologists seek proof (Gotham, 2004) that one particular approach is superior to another! Kilburg (2004: 207) sums this position up very well – '*I find it somewhat ironic, intellectually puzzling, and paradoxically reassuring that after a century of trying to specify the effectiveness of psychotherapy, the field now finds itself dealing with the major empirical conclusion that the differences between approaches would appear to be nil but nevertheless positive for patients across problem conditions*'. This does not mean that either the research or the intervention is wrong or does not work, but it does suggest that the common element is that human beings like to engage with each other, talk to each other, and help each other, and generally we find this therapeutic and beneficial. So what's wrong with that?

For me, there seems a familiar chime within the coaching psychology world on research. I have recently examined three coaching PhD theses from three different countries, all of which were positivistic studies from psychology departments and all of which had inconclusive conclusions that called for further research! Last year, I also examined a thesis on mentoring conducted in the same way with the same conclusion! So psychotherapy works and so does coaching and I really do think that they do – but not necessarily all the time and who decides what 'works' actually means?

Probably because of the increase in academic qualifications for coaches delivered by universities or accredited by universities, there is a growing body of research of varying quality beginning to emerge and this work is finding its way into coaching-based journals, general management journals, psychology journals, and books. It is, however, interesting that these new discourses are more forthcoming from the psychology of coaching world than from anywhere else.

To speculate for a moment, this may be because psychology is a recognised academic discipline and therefore a research base is necessary. It may also be an attempt to strengthen and differentiate the coaching psychology brand in a crowded marketplace. The dominant discourse of positivism as the only scientific way of proceeding is deeply embedded in this context and perhaps psychologists and coaching psychologists are stuck in a repetitive narrative.

I predict that in the next five years there will be a plethora of positivistic research of varying quality in the coaching and coaching psychology world and all of it will not be fully proven and inconclusive or at least open to critical debate and disagreement.

So where does that leave coaching education?

Berglas (2002: 89) thinks that a knowledge of psychology is necessary in coaching and asserts that only trained therapists should coach. However, his position seems split when he states:

> My misgivings about executive coaching are not a clarion call for psychotherapy and psychoanalysis. Psychoanalysis, in particular, does not – and will never – suit everybody. Nor is it up to corporate leaders to ensure that all employees deal with their personal demons. My goal, as somebody with a doctorate in psychology as well as serving as an executive coach, is to heighten awareness of the difference between a problem executive, who can be trained to function effectively, and an executive with a problem who can best be helped by psychotherapy ...'

So what does Berglas mean here? Is coaching informed by psychology or not? Should it be? Do we need *'personal demons'* to benefit from it? Is he emphasising that having a doctorate strengthens his position and provides credibility?

Lee (2003) offers some help when he refers to *'psychological mindedness'* as an important element of a coach's practice. Bluckert (2006: 87) describes this as *'people's capacity to reflect on themselves, others, and the relationship in between'* and argues that this is best done with an understanding and awareness of psychological processes.

Dean and Meyer (2002: 12) are much more assertive in their statement that psychological training *'will assure that the coach has the basic knowledge and clinical skills needed to accomplish the objectives and goals'*.

On the other side of this debate Filipczak (1998: 203) believes that psychological training for coaches is *'potentially harmful'*. This is mainly because a psychologist may not have any understanding of the business environment and could have a tendency to see a business *'as another dysfunctional family that needs to be fixed'* (1998: 34) – a similar issue to the positive psychology debate, or if you *'only have a hammer everything looks like a nail!'* (This saying is attributed to Abraham Maslow but I cannot find any direct written reference.)

There is also the issue of fees. Bono et al. (2009) show that psychologists who coach charge higher fees than 'ordinary coaches' and receive up to 50% of their income from coaching. This seems to suggest that there are also commercial interests here as psychologists may see a way to increase their earning potential if they move into coaching: the calls for psychological training from psychologists may be protectionist in nature – another power play from a partisan group?

what is the psychology of mentoring discourse?

The psychological training and discourses coming from the psychology world are more muted within the mentoring literature. This is not to say that mentoring does not draw from psychology to help frame itself and create a body of knowledge. Within the mentoring discourse, psychological frameworks are often employed as part of theory building.

As first raised in Chapter 1, Kram stated that mentoring performs a 'psychosocial function' (1983: 616). This suggests that it offers both a socialising process within a specific social context and it develops self-insight and psychological wellbeing. Kram and other US researchers, for example, Belle Rose Ragins, Terri Scanudra, Monica Higgins and Dawn Chandler, often examined the learning and development elements within mentoring, as have Alred et al. (1998), Johnson et al. (1999) and Moberg and Velasquez (2004).

Beech and Brockbank (1999) employ ideas drawn from psychosocial dynamics to look at issues of power within mentoring relationships. Aryree and Chay (1994) examine issues of commitment and career satisfaction within mentoring while McAuley (2003) employs the psychodynamic notion of transference and countertransference within mentoring relationships and presents these as issues of power dynamics within the relationship. Morgan and Davidson (2008) and Erdem and Aytemur (2008) look at various other issues that relate to relationship dynamics, for example trust and gender issues. Turban and Dougherty (1994) employ the concept of personality types within mentoring and Emmerik (2008) looks at the issue performance with mentoring. Colley (2002) emphasises emotional support for mentees as a challenge for mentors who are engaged in and challenged by the emotional labour of mentoring. Several writers, for example Levinson et al. (1978), Ragins and Scandura (1994), Johnson et al. (1999), Moberg and Velasquez (2004), link mentoring activity to the psychological concept of 'generativity' (Erikson, 1978).

These are just a few examples of where mentoring employs psychological underpinning to build theory and explain this. For me, this places mentoring primarily within the developmental psychology domain and not within the domain that preoccupies the coaching literature – the psychotherapeutic.

Also, within the mentoring literature, a research base is more established. Much of this is US research – largely survey-based and positivistic studies. However, there are also many case studies and consultant-led studies that add to the overall discourse about mentoring. This provides a rich picture of mentoring activity and while, as outlined in previous chapters, mentoring activity is not without its challenges – for example, power issues, manipulation, dysfunctional and abusive behaviour and ethical issues – the concerns about psychological training for mentors are not present. Perhaps this is because mentoring are often positioned as voluntary, often without fees being involved, and allegedly altruistic as raised in Chapters 3 and 4.

bringing things together

Within the domains of coaching and mentoring, the psychological concepts of meaning and sense making are central and this is what unites them. However, the psychology world has built its foundation on a positivistic, cause and effect philosophy that in my opinion is based on a medical model of research. Here is the problem; three major issues in this model of research govern its operation:

1. The researcher is neutral and objective.
2. It is important to isolate variables in order to know what you are testing.
3. Coaching, mentoring and psychotherapy are not static, they are dynamic processes and change occurs all the time.

With human activity, Skolimowski (1992: 42) sums up my position very well when he considers that objectivity in human affairs is '*a figment of our minds; it does not exist in nature*'. The second point creates huge problems in mentoring, coaching and psychological research. In many ways, isolating variables in human activity is virtually impossible and often this is fudged through the introduction of control group studies and clever statistical calculations – it is this that leads to inconclusive conclusions. The fact that human relationships are dynamic also creates a problem because positivism tends towards treating human relationships as static and therefore the results often become a fixed point in time rather than a narrative for change.

Bruner (1990: 32), a psychologist himself, challenges the psychology world about its underpinning philosophy:

> Psychology … deals only in objective truths and eschews cultural criticism. But even scientific psychology will fare better when it recognises that its truths about the human condition are relative to the point of view that it takes toward that condition.

He also states (1990: 33) that 'meaning' is a central notion within human psychology and suggests that '*we shall be able to interpret meanings and meaning-making in a principled manner only in the degree to which we are able to specify the structure and coherence of the larger contexts in which specific meanings are created and transmitted*' (1990: 64). We are social beings and the social environments we inhabit therefore influence our identity, attitudes, thoughts, feelings and behaviours. In other words, it is only possible to make any sense of the human condition if we take into account the context in which the individual or group is located: thus controlling the human dynamic variable is not possible.

Bruner (1996: 39) goes further in a later work when he states *'there appear to be two broad ways in which human beings organize and manage their knowledge of the world, indeed structure even their immediate experience: one seems more specialized for treating of physical "things" the other for treating of people and their plights. They are conventionally thought of as logical-scientific thinking and narrative thinking'*.

This is a clear acknowledgement that there cannot be only one-way and Bruner's two organising concepts are of equal significance and need to be taken into account when observing and interpreting human behaviour. Bruner (1990: 33) bases his assertion upon two linked arguments. Namely, that to understand people it is important to understand how their experiences and actions are shaped by their *'intentional states'* and that the form these take is realised through the *'participation in the symbolic systems of the culture'*. He states that it is the surrounding culture and external environment, and not biological factors, which shape the human life and mind. They do this by imposing the patterns inherent in the culture's symbolic systems *'its language and discourse modes, the forms of logical and narrative explication, and the patterns of mutually dependent communal life'*. Therefore, in any investigation into coaching and mentoring – social processes in themselves – it is crucial to interpret language, symbols and myths in the context of the environment in which they applied. If this is the case, the human understanding of universal 'truth' is challenged and the concept of alethic pluralism raised in Chapters 1 and 2 and discussed throughout starts to offer a way forward.

In practical terms alethic pluralism can inform the development of competencies, approaches to the education of coaches and mentors, evaluation and research. For example, within the competency and educational arenas for coach and mentor development this could translate into a *'repertoire'* (Garvey et al., 2009) approach. This would mean that coaches and mentors would need more than one framework to work with and as suggested in Chapter 1 both coaching and mentoring draw on many subject disciplines and no one has a monopoly on good or best practice. Therefore to be psychologically minded seems appropriate as one element of coach/mentor development. Other disciplines (see Chapter 1) apart from psychology can contribute to avoid a 'one size fits all' approach or a dominating discourse and, more importantly, this will enable the coachee or mentee to benefit from a tailored approach that is able to meet his or her needs. However, as discussed in Chapter 5, this alternative position remains a sadly weak discourse as the coaching and to some extent the mentoring worlds seem to want to differentiate position and brand.

In sum, with reference to psychology, within the coaching discourse there continues to be more positioning and differentiating going on than within the mentoring discourse where psychology is generally used to help build theory within a developmental discourse. This serves to further illustrate a social phenomenon raised in Chapters 1 and 3 that none of these discourses is neutral and by seeking to differentiate here – often by elevating one position and denigrating another – the diversity perspective is driven out to the detriment of mentoring and coaching practice.

7

Conclusions and Further Questions

introduction

This chapter brings together the themes of the book and attempts to extract some meaning and extend some thoughts from previous chapters. It also raises some further questions.

history

Mentoring activity has a long and fairly well documented history that is traceable to Ancient Greece. It is associated with one-to-one learning and development, leadership development and social integration. With the development of education in the eighteenth century, a number of books drew on the Ancient Greek story to illustrate the process. In more recent times, mentoring has started to be employed in a range of social and occupational settings. There are many variations of application and intent across the world.

Coaching, as a term, is traceable to Oxford University where it was employed as part of the one-to-one learning philosophy that persists there to enhance academic performance. The term was also employed in relation to sport and life skills.

In recent years, coaching has grown as a commercial activity across many developed and developing economies. Mentoring has tended to remain a voluntary activity aimed at learning and development within specific social contexts.

Research (Willis, 2005) clearly shows that both coaching and mentoring share the same skills sets and processes. However, where they differ is in context and purpose. Moreover, and despite their similarity, there seems to be many different definitions and descriptions of coaching and mentoring and considerable positioning and posturing as to the differences both within the literature and among the practitioner community. Much of this is influenced by commercial or philosophical interests. What is clear is that within the coaching world there is strong discussion about coaching as a profession, and also coaching as a line management 'tool'. The line manager coaching agenda has yet to address ethical issues, questions of manipulation and power dynamics.

Mentoring tends to be a voluntary activity and the potential power differentials between mentor and mentee appear to be minimised in many organisational schemes by creating cross-functional rather than line relationships. However, power issues are still present within mentoring.

Overall, I would conclude that both are indeed similar and social and therefore subject to social dynamics and change. Neither coaching nor mentoring, in my view, could be described as scientific and the concept of alethic pluralism, as discussed in Chapters 1 and 2, offers the possibility that coaching and mentoring are an eclectic mix though often with a similar intent – learning, development and performance improvement.

historical linkage

There is also considerable linkage in the literature to history. As far as my research has gone, the only direct link to ancient history is found with the use of the term 'mentoring'. The motivations for this historical linkage within the coaching discourse are not always clear but it may be an attempt to establish credibility or to refute the claim that coaching is a modern fad. In any case, Nietzsche (1873) was of the opinion that studying history was a worthless activity and, if it must be studied, it should not be devoid of the context that gave it life – we must judge history in terms of the context in which it happened!

The history of the term 'coaching' in the English language is directly linked to the nineteenth century in England. Therefore, it is a more recent term. However, some writers make the claim that coaching is derived from Socratic dialogue. While there are some similarities to the Socratic method found in mentoring and coaching practice – for example, detailed questioning, seeking truth and consensus – overall, Socratic dialogue seemed to have a different purpose to coaching and mentoring and, as argued by Nietzsche, the concept may have been responsible for the destruction of creative mythology (see Chapter 2). Perhaps this was also the start of rational pragmatism and positivism.

rational pragmatism

As a concept and way of behaving, a premise of this book is that Western management is dominated by the concept of the 'pragmatic, rational manager'. This manager attempts to control and manage the complex human system of the organisation using rational and pragmatic approaches and while this approach has been responsible for great progress in social, economic and scientific advances it can break down as the results are unpredictable. Predictability is fast becoming a redundant concept in the complex world of business.

Positivism is the conventional academic mode. It is an empirical approach, which is based on a systematic accumulation of 'facts'. It draws its strength from an alleged theoretically neutral observation language. This language assumes rationality which suggests that people and their behaviours can be explained deterministically. This very dominant mode of thinking has been a driver of the modern industrialised world, with the resultant knowledge being *'characterized by a form of rationality that disengages the mind from the body and from the world'* (Apffel-Marglin & Marglin, 1996: 3). This notion is clearly inappropriate in the study of coaching and mentoring for four main reasons:

1. The conditions and environments in which the research takes place are varied and complex and therefore indeterminate.
2. Coaching is under-theorised and mentoring, while it is researched extensively, is the same. The nature of coaching and mentoring means that deriving any application of theoretical generalisations in the research would have to be made *post hoc*.
3. Since any generalisation must be drawn from a sample, there would be a statistical generalisation stating a property of a particular direction or size which can only be meaningfully assessed within its own statistical boundaries. The statistics themselves become self-limiting.
4. Positivistic studies are rooted in a deductive method which sets out from an established body of knowledge to test and prove. The pre-specification necessary here can only engineer what has been pre-specified. Coaching and mentoring are, in themselves, developmental journeys whose outcome may be unclear but the travellers may well be enriched by their very travelling – as raised in Chapter 6 – as they are dynamic.

Whilst it may be argued (Apffel-Marglin & Marglin, 1996: 2) that a dominant deterministic logic has been responsible for much progress in terms of industrial development, it could also be said that it is also responsible for *'social fragmentation'* and *'environmental destruction'* (Apeffel-Marglin and Marglin, 1996: 2). Science has created environmental and social problems on an epic scale! It has, for example, given rise to an unhelpful mindset towards people within the management community.

The positivist approach to knowledge acquisition, with its roots in Newtonian scientific methodology, is underpinned by the idea of 'rightness'.

However, this is breaking down: *'there is no longer a "right knowledge", but many coexisting conflicting pieces of knowledge'* (Von Krogh et al., 1994: 54), and *'Sociological positivism's strict emulation of the natural sciences has been tried and its benefits have now been exhausted'* (Reed & Harvey, 1992: 354) for *'Positivist canons can suffice only in the closed domain of the experimental setting'* (Reed & Harvey, 1992: 356).

The work of the philosopher Roy Bhaskar (see Reed & Harvey, 1992: 356–357) has contributed substantially to this debate. He presents three main principles:

- 'Experimental method is neither a self contained nor a self-sufficient technique for discovering causal laws'.
- 'For positivism to sustain a plausible self-accounting, it must abandon empirical realism and ground its explanations in a world of entities – entities that are endowed with real causal powers, latent capacities, and slumbering liabilities'.
- 'Science is a social activity'.

In the social science context, the assumption of 'predictability' or 'determinism' is now increasingly being challenged in other quarters (Parker & Stacey, 1994). It is widely accepted (Apffel-Marglin and Marglin, 1993, 1996; Reed & Harvey, 1992; Senge, 1992; Stacey, 1995) that research, driven by the quest for knowledge and understanding, is a highly complex series of dependencies and variables and it is crucial to try to extract 'meaning' (see Bruner, 1990) holistically from the complex situation under investigation.

> the determinists dream of mathematically precise predictability at all times and in all places has given way to ... qualitative predictions of the asymptotic behaviour of the system in the long run. (Abraham & Shaw, 1982: 27)

Clearly, a range of methodologies is appropriate to extract meaning from complex social situations such as coaching and mentoring. A 'new' methodology, aimed at fully exploring knowledge which is *'complex, emergently-structured and multi-layered* [in a] *universe of discrete entities and mechanisms'* (Reed & Harvey, 1992: 358), becomes appropriate.

The following quote about research methodology could apply to the discourses found in coaching and mentoring.

> When we wonder about something, we not only need to look for answers to questions never asked before, we need to become inventive about ways of finding out things. Otherwise, methodology may

> become a severe constraint on the degree of novelty in the knowledge produced. (Von Krogh et al., 1994: 54)

The concept of alethic pluralism discussed throughout the book offers such an alternative and mixed approach to researching coaching and mentoring. I am by no means suggesting that this is a simpler alternative – in many ways empirical studies are easier than this approach but that should not stop researchers working with such concepts in order to think new thoughts.

At this point it is time to bring together the espoused theory of coaching and mentoring and start to actually live it (Argyris, 1992)!

the economics and challenges of learning and development

As raised in Chapter 4, there is not only a social but also an economic reason for organisations placing value on learning and development. Often it is unique knowledge that enables strategic progress and a step change. In my view, it is not possible to conceive of a form of human economic life that is not based on specialised knowledge of some kind.

Pre-industrial economies relied on simple, human or animal-powered technology and the craft skills and understanding associated with their use. From the fifteenth and sixteenth centuries onwards, global trade and, later, industrialism, brought new skills, science and technology and profound changes to the fabric of commercial, financial, legal and political life. Indeed, they fashioned an entirely new order of human society and experience.

There are two ideas that capture this – modernity and complexity.

Modernity highlights the driving force of ideas such as progress, the rational organisation of society, democracy and ever-higher living standards. It encodes within itself the perhaps mistaken belief that human beings can achieve a rational control of their lives and the future development of their societies. I suggest that the notion of modernity is waning in the light of an accelerating complexity.

Complexity captures a key feature of both: the growth of new ideas, knowledge and understanding, driven forward by science and scholarship. Complexity, by definition, is ultimately unmanageable. Not only are social and economic changes always one step ahead of our knowledge, new knowledge also reflects back on the ways in which human societies are organised and change. Soros (2000) characterises this phenomenon as reflexivity.

The kinds of conversation that take place in mentoring and coaching sessions, potentially at least, are the stuff of reflexivity. For me, this is where a real potential for coaching and mentoring sits and it is also where we need to invest our energies.

supercomplexity and reflexivity

The concept of complexity in social affairs, as argued by Barnett (2000), is giving way to a new supercomplexity. Supercomplexity defines an intellectual universe devoid of certainty and one that is essentially open to new ideas and ways of thinking.

The concepts of supercomplexity and reflexivity present entirely new challenges to those responsible for managing our organisations. The comments raised in the Introduction to this book about a desire, so often found in organisations, to simplify the complex is just one of these. Of more concern is the outcome that unless managers and leaders themselves are tuned to the supercomplexity of their circumstances and actively pursue novel ideas and ways to solve current problems, they will be left behind in the economy of ideas. However, as the banking crisis showed us, new ideas when unregulated can be ethically dubious and downright dangerous. In my view the dominant discourse of deregulation and free markets created this problem and if this goes unchecked it will create more in the future. Hutton's (1997) prophecy quoted in the Introduction has come true. Reflexivity, if applied to the banking crisis, offers the potential to think new thoughts and do different things. Sadly, the old ways seem to be creeping back into bankers' ways of thinking and this is why there is a problem with Blakey and Day's (2009) contribution as was raised in the Introduction.

Curiously, I agree with Blakey and Day that coaching (and mentoring) offer the potential to address some of the issues raised by the concept of supercomplexity (they do not use this term) and could help to develop a more reflexive way forward for executives within the banking sector. However, I would disagree with what seem to be their motivations which, in my view, simply mirror the unregulated, free market philosophy that led to the crisis. However, the espoused values of coaching and mentoring offer some hope that a new order can be created, even if the capacity to make this paradigm change is not uniformly developed either throughout nations, among the organisations of economic life, nor sadly among the coaching and mentoring community.

Our insistence on going to war to resolve difficulties and violence to make our voices heard is a very primitive behaviour. These aggressive tendencies are manifest in bankers' threats to move elsewhere if the rules change – this is free market, survival of the fittest thinking.

We can live in space, cure many diseases, communicate across the globe in seconds – but we still somehow resort to baser behaviour in the face of competition. The managers of those organisations – nation states, corporations, public services, voluntary groups – who nurture in their colleagues critical awareness, acceptance and tolerance and reduce power and control obsessions are the ones who are most likely to become successful in this new supercomplex world. They will be the organisations that are best able to handle knowledge and information, to act on it, and be sufficiently geared up to keep abreast of the changes taking place around them. The rest will just try to slug it out in the same old ways!

Coaching and mentoring are about achieving dynamic changes for individuals. I believe that this is possible and that it is also possible to achieve change at an organisational level because I have seen a glimpse of this in those organizations who do try to work differently.

emancipatory, speculative and performative knowledge

In Chapter 1, I raised Lyotard's (1984) three elements of knowledge and in Chapter 2 showed how much of what is constructed in organisational settings is focused on the 'performative'. For me this is not just a missed opportunity to develop both the 'speculative' and 'emancipatory' – essential if knowledge is a key driver of economic progress. The slogan of the French revolution, *liberté, égalité, fraternité*, has yet to be realised in organisational life. Personally speaking, this is a huge paradox. So-called developed countries go to war to defend democracy or impose it on others and yet our economic powerhouses are simply undemocratic! Coaching and mentoring offer the opportunity for people to think new thoughts and therefore to liberate themselves from repeating the errors of the past as if they have learned nothing from them. This, in turn, could lead to great emancipation.

discourses

The concept of dominant discourse is a theme employed throughout this book. Coaching and mentoring conversations deal with both these elements and herein lies a further potential. As stated by all the authors quoted in Chapter 1 from the eighteenth century, by bringing together the emotional and the rational, new insights and understanding can chime together and this can lead to new behaviours. However, as Bohm (1996: 3) states in relation to one-to-one dialogue *'but of course, such communication can lead to the creation of something new only if people are able freely to listen to each other, without prejudice, and without trying to influence each other. Each has to be interested primarily in truth and coherence, so that he is ready to drop his old ideas and intentions, and be ready to go on to something different, when this is called for'*. This leads to another theme in the book, the discourse of power.

Management power and control is an inherent assumption within rational pragmatic discourse and this is often the source of social problems in the workplace. Coaching and mentoring activity can offer the prospect of enabling new thoughts and as social processes these aim to reduce power and control by handing power to the coachee and mentee. However, this is not only difficult to achieve it is also often a false assumption and potentially a fake conversation.

Language is part of a power discourse (Layder, 1994) and discourses influence the practice of both coaching and mentoring as discussed in Chapters 2 and 3. In Chapter 4, I raised the issue of professionalisation as a power discourse. In my view, this does not have to be the case and if coaching and mentoring are to stay an eclectic mix of practices, the much-espoused values that underpin these social activities need to remain dominant in people's minds. Researchers and professional bodies need to present this case by living the professed values of coaching and mentoring – trusting, valuing the relationship, exploring possibilities and options, challenging assumptions and equality – to mention but a few. This is what offers the potential for change and not positioning, branding, controlling and differentiating.

However, as George Eliot wrote in the classic novel *Adam Bede*: *'Examine your words well, and you will find that even when you have no motive to be false, it is a very hard thing to say the exact truth, even about your own immediate feelings – much harder than t'say something fine about them which is not the exact truth'* (1997[1859]: 223).

This is another example of the notion that in human affairs there are often not falsehoods or lies, but alternative meanings. Concepts of 'rightness' or 'wrongness' are, in my view, just too basic. As people we can be more sophisticated than that and coaching and mentoring activity has the potential to work with meaning and assist new ones to develop. This is another potential power of a one-to-one development conversation.

Coaching and mentoring take us *'into the realms of capability building where people are able to exercise judgements, make decisions and develop wisdom in their work. Here, ideas of "one best way", "singing from the same hymn sheet" and the like seem rather simplistic objectives – an optimistic misjudgement of the reality of the workplace'* (Garvey & Williamson, 2002: 87).

and the future?

I have tried to show throughout this book that there are many aspects to coaching and mentoring activity, many versions, many stories, and a great deal of posturing and positioning. In essence, the kinds of conversation that are potentially open to us are many and varied and, if they are to be productive, these need to be conducted in the spirit of openness and trust and with reduced power distinctions. Any other way will inevitably lead to difficulties. In short, coaching and mentoring conversations are conversations with a purpose and the purpose is often some kind of change.

Recent discussions about the future of organisations place the concepts of knowledge and experience of older employees, complemented by the indispensable abilities and imagination of newcomers, as central to organisational progress (Prahalad & Bettis, 1996). Starkey (1998: 534) identified the essence of leadership as *'senior executives' ability to distinguish between knowing what they still have to contribute and recognising what they need to learn from others'*. There is a creative tension between learning from the past and unlearning for the future. In many ways coaching and mentoring, as discussed in this book, provide a way forward in helping organisations to meet the challenges of today in an arena in which the tension between a known past and an unknown future can be profitably exploited in a knowledge productive and reflexive present.

For me, this challenge is a serious one because both coaching and mentoring activity can be helpful for all people in the workplace. They have the potential to help people tolerate the increasing complexity of their personal and working lives. However, coaching and mentoring, being complex, are not always readily accepted or understood. As said before, they can be readily simplified but the risk is that the great potential for change and thinking new thoughts remains untapped. Were a connoisseur of wine to discuss coaching and mentoring and the appreciation of complex vintages, their argument would have parallels with what I have sketched throughout this book. The connoisseured may prefer the term 'fine' rather than 'complex', and they may describe the challenges of coaching and mentoring as the avoidance of yet one more coarsened and oversimplified palate.

Coaching and mentoring cannot be 'cure-alls' for every organisational ill or social problem and from my experience they are least effective when viewed as a 'new initiative' rather than natural processes and parts of normal behaviour at work. This view brings with it a risk that by themselves coaching and mentoring have the potential to be neutral with regard to fundamental organisational change and at the same time can initiate, facilitate and support change. They could, in equal measure, promote change or conserve the status quo. As with all human activities coaching and mentoring are flawed, but that does not negate their potential for improving all our lives. Human beings can be brilliant at relationships and also rubbish at them at the same time! In my opinion it is time to think new thoughts, embrace the diverse world with energy and enthusiasm, and give up the unhelpful thoughts of the past that still so dominate our mindsets. Happy thinking!

And to close;

> If one is truly to succeed in leading a person to a specific place, one must first and foremost take care to find him where he is and begin there. This is the secret in the entire art of helping. Anyone who cannot do this is himself under a delusion in he thinks he is able to help someone else. In order truly to help someone else, I must understand more than he – but certainly first and foremost understand what he understands. If I do not do that, then my greater understanding does not help him at all. If I nevertheless want to assert my greater understanding, then it is because I am vain or proud, then basically instead of benefiting him I really want to be admired by him. But all true helping begins with a humbling. The helper must first humble himself under the person he wants to help and thereby understand that to help is not to dominate but to serve, that to help is a willingness for the time being to put up with being wrong and not understanding what the other understands. (Kierkegaard, 1998)

References

books and journals

Abraham, R.A. and Shaw, C.D. (1982) *Dynamics, the Geometry of Behaviour, Part One: Periodic Behaviour.* Santa Cruz, CA: Ariel Press.

Allen, T.D., Eby, L.T., Poteet, M.L., Lentz, E. and Lima, L. (2004) Career benefits associated with mentoring for protégés: a meta-analysis, *Journal of Applied Psychology,* 89(4): 127–138.

Alred, G. and Garvey, B. (2010) The *Mentoring Pocket Book*, 3rd edn. Management Pocket Book Series: Mentoring. Hampshire Arlesford Press.

Alred, G., Garvey, B. and Smith, R.D. (1998) Pas de deux: learning in conversations, *Career Development International*, 3(7): 308–314.

Amabile, T. (1997) Motivating creativity in organizations: on doing what you love and loving what you do, *California Management Review,* 40: 39–58.

Apffel-Marglin, F. and Marglin, S.A. (1993) *Dominating Knowledge: Development, Culture and Resistance.* Oxford: Clarendon Press.

Appffel-Marglin, F. and Marglin, S.A. (1996) *Decolonizing Knowledge: From Development to Dialogue.* Oxford: Clarendon Press.

Argyris, C. (1992) *On Organizational Learning*. Malden, MA: Blackwell Publishing.

Argyris, C. and Schon, D.A. (1981) *Organizational Learning*. Reading, MA: Addison-Wesley.

Arnaud, G. (2003) A coach or a couch? A Lacanian perspective on executive coaching and consulting, *Human Relations,* 56(9): 1131–1154.

Aryree, S. and Chay, Y.W. (1994) An examination of the impact of career-oriented mentoring on work commitment attitudes and career satisfaction among professional and managerial employees, *British Journal of Management,* 5: 241–249.

Back, L. (2004) Ivory towers? The academy and racism. In I. Law, D. Phillips and L. Turney (eds), *Institutional Racism in Higher Education.* Stoke on Trent: Trentham Books.

Bandura, A. (1977) Self-efficacy: toward a unifying theory of behavioral change, *Psychological Review*, 84(2): 191–215.

Barnett, R. (1994) *The Limits of Competence: Knowledge, Higher Education, and Society.* Buckingham: SRHE/Open University Press.

Barnett, R. (2000) Working knowledge. In J. Garrick and C. Rhodes (eds), *Research and Knowledge at Work*. pp. 15–32. London: Routledge.

Barrett, F.J. (1998) Managing and improvising: lessons from jazz. *Career Development International*, 3(7): 283–286.

Bauman, Z. (1989) *Modernity and the Holocaust*. Cambridge: Polity.

Beech, N. and Brockbank, A. (1999) Power/knowledge and psychosocial dynamics in mentoring, *Management Learning*, 30(1): 7–25.

Bell, E., Taylor, S. and Thorpe, R. (2002) A step in the right direction? Investors in people and the learning organisation, *British Journal of Management*, 13: 161–171.

Berglas, S. (2002) The very real dangers of executive coaching, *Harvard Business Review*, June: 3–8.

Berman, E.M. and West, J.P. (2008) Managing emotional intelligence in US cities: a study of social skills among public managers, *Public Administration Review*, July/August: 742–758.

Bernstein, B. (1971) On the classification and framing of educational knowledge. In M.F.D. Young (ed.), *Knowledge and Control: New Directions for the Sociology of Education*. pp. 47–69. London: Open University, Collier-MacMillan.

Bhavnani, R., Mirza, H.S. and Meetoo, V. (2005) *Tackling the Roots of Racism: Lessons for Success*. Bristol: Policy Press.

Biswas-Diener, R. and Dean, B. (2007) *Positive Psychology Coaching: Putting the Science of Happiness to Work for Your Clients*. Hoboken, NJ: John Wiley.

Blakey, J. and Day, I. (2009) *Where Were all the Coaches When the Banks Went Down?* 121 Partners Ltd., UK.

Bluckert, P. (2006) *Psychological Dimensions of Executive Coaching*. Maidenhead: Open University Press.

Bohm, D. (1996) *On Dialogue*. London: Routledge.

Boisot, M., Lemmon, T., Griffiths, D. and Mole, V. (1996) Spinning a good yarn: the identification of core competencies at Courtaulds. *International Journal of Technology Management*. Special Issue on the 5th International Forum on Technology Management. Vol. 11, Nos. 3/4: 425–440.

Bolden, R. and Gosling, J. (2006) Leadership competencies: time to change the tune? *Leadership*, 2: 147–163.

Bono, J.E., Purvanova, R.K., Towler, A.J. and Peterson, D. (2009) A survey of executive coaching practices, *Personnel Psychology*, 62: 361–404.

Bowen, D.D. (1985) Were men meant to mentor women? *Training and Development Journal*, 36 February: 30–34.

Broad, M.L. and Newstom, J.W. (1992) *Transfer of Training: Action-Packed Strategies to Ensure a High Payoff from Training Investments*. Reading, MA: Addison-Wesley.

Brockbank, A. and McGill, I. (2006) *Facilitating Reflective Learning through Mentoring and Coaching*. London: Kogan Page.

Brown, C.D. (1993) Male/female mentoring: turning potential risks into rewards, *IEEE Transactions on Professional Communication*, 36(4): 197–201.

Brundrett, M. (2000) The question of competence: the origins, strengths and inadequacies of a leadership training paradigm, *School Leadership and Management*, 20(3): 353–369.

Bruner, J. (1990) *Acts of Meaning*. Harvard, MA: Harvard University Press.

Bruner, J. (1996) *The Culture of Education*. Harvard, MA: Harvard University Press.

Brunner, R. (1998) Psychoanalysis and Coaching, *Journal of Management Psychology*, 13(7): 515–517.

Brunning, H. (2006). The six domains of executive coaching. In H. Brunning (ed.), *Executive Coaching: Systems-psychodynamic Perspective*. pp. 131–151. London: Karnac Books.

Buber, M. (1958) Teaching and deed. In W. Herberg (ed.), *The Writings of Martin Buber*. Meridian Books, USA.

Caraccioli, L.A. (1760) *The True Mentor, or, An Essay on the Education of Young People in Fashion*. J. Coote at the King's Arms in Paternoster Row, London.

Carden, A. (1990) Mentoring and adult career development, *The Counselling Psychologist*, 18(2): 275–299.

Carmin, C.N. (1988) Issues in research on mentoring: definitional and methodological, *International Journal of Mentoring*, 2(2): 9–13.

Carroll, M. (2003) The new kid on the block, *Counselling Psychotherapy Journal*, December 14/10: 28–31.

Caulkin, S. (1995) The Measure Principal. *The Observer*, 30 July.

Caulkin, S. (1997) League tables? A restaurant guide is a lot more use. *The Observer*, 6 April.

Chadwick-Coule, T. and Garvey, B. (2009) *London Deanery Mentoring Service: A Formative and Developmental Evaluation of Working Practices and Outcomes*, The Coaching and Mentoring Research Unit, Sheffield Business School, Sheffield Hallam University.

Chapman, L. (2010) *Integrated Experiential Coaching: Becoming an Executive Coach*. London: Karnac.

Clawson, J.G. (1996) Mentoring in the Information Age, *Leadership and Organization Development Journal*, 17(3): 6–15.

Clawson, J.G. and Kram, K.E. (1984) Managing cross-gender mentoring, *Business Horizons*, May–June: 22–32.

Clutterbuck, D. (1998) *Learning Alliances: Tapping into Talent.* London: Institute of Personnel and Development.

Clutterbuck, D. (2004) *Everyone Needs a Mentor.* London: The Chartered Institute of Personnel and Development.

Clutterbuck, D. (2007) An International Perspective on Mentoring. In B.R., Ragins and K.E. Kram (eds), *Handbook on Mentoring at Work: Theory, Research and Practice.* Thousand Oaks, CA: Sage.

Clutterbuck, D. and Lane, G. (2004) *The Situational Mentor.* Aldershot: Gower Publishing.

Clutterbuck, D. and Megginson, D. (1999) *Mentoring Executives and Directors.* Oxford: Butterworth-Heinemann.

Clutterbuck, D. and Megginson, D. (2005) *Making Coaching Work, Creating a Coaching Culture.* London: The Chartered Institute of Personnel and Development.

Colley, H. (2002) A 'Rough Guide' to the history of mentoring from a marxist feminist perspective, *Journal of Education for Teaching,* 28(3): 247–263.

Colley, H. (2003) *Mentoring For Social Inclusion: A Critical Approach to Nurturing Relationships.* London: RoutledgeFalmer.

Cox, E. (2006) An adult learning approach to coaching. In D. Stober, and A. Grant (eds), *The Handbook* of *Evidence Based Coaching.* Chichester: Wiley.

Cox, E. and Ledgerwood, G. (2003) 'The new profession', *International Journal of Evidence Based Coaching and Mentoring,* 1(1).

Cox, E., Bachkirova, T. and Clutterbuck, D. (2010) *The Complete Handbook of Coaching.* London: Sage.

Cullen, E. (1992) A vital way to manage change, *Education,* 13 November: 3–17.

Darwin, J. (2010) Kuhn vs. Popper vs. Lakatos vs. Feyerabend: contested terrain or fruitful collaboration? Unpublished, Sheffield Hallam University.

Davies, B.R. (1999) Prospects for mentoring in dentistry, *Medical Teacher,* 21(3): 322–323.

Dean, M.L. and Meyer A.A. (2002) Executive coaching: in search of a model, *Journal of Leadership Education,* 1: 1–15.

Dembkowski, S. and Eldridge, F. (2003) Beyond GROW: a new coaching model, *International Journal of Mentoring and Coaching,* 1(1).

de Haan, E. (2008) *Relational Coaching: Journeys towards Mastering One-to-One Learning.* Chichester: John Wiley.

De La Mothe-Fenelon, F.S. (1808) *The Adventures of Telemachus,* Vols 1 and 2. London: Union Printing Office.

De Meuse, K.P. and Dai, G. (2008) *Does Executive Coaching Work? A Research Analysis*. Lominger International, A Korn/Ferry Company.
Dewey, J. (1958) *Experience and Nature*. New York: Dover Publications.
Dougherty, D.T. (1994) Role of protègè personality in receipt of mentoring and career success, *Academy of Management Journal*, 37(3): 688–702.
Downey, M. (2003) *Effective Coaching*. London: Texere.
Drucker, P.F. (1992) *Managing in a Time of Great Change*. Oxford: Butterworth–Heinemann.
Ecclestone, K. (1997) Energising or enervating implications of National Vocational Qualifications in professional development, *Journal of Vocational Education and Training*, 49: 65–79.
Egan, G. (1993) *Adding Value: A Systematic Guide to Business-Driven Management and Leadership*. Hoboken, NJ: Jossey-Bass.
Ehrenreich, B. (2009) *Smile or Die: How Positive Thinking Fooled America and the World*. London: Granta Books.
Eliot, G. (1997) (first published 1859) *Adam Bede*. Harmondsworth: Penguin.
Elliot, A.J. and Conroy, D.E. (2005) Beyond the dichotomous model of achievement goals in sport and exercise psychology, *Sport & Exercise Psychology Review*, 1(1): 17–25.
Emmerik, I.J. (2008) It is not only mentoring: the combined influences of individual-level and team-level support on job performance, *Career Development International*, 13(7): 575–593.
Erdem, F. and Aytemur, J.O. (2008) Mentoring – a relationship based on trust: qualitative, *Research Public Personnel Management*, 37(1): 55–65.
Erikson, E. (1978) *Childhood and Society*. Harmondsworth: Penguin.
Evers, W.J.G., Brouwers, A. and Tomic, W. (2006) A quasi-experimental study on management coaching effectiveness, *Consulting Psychology Journal: Practice & Research Review*, 58(3): 174–182.
Filipczak, B. (1998) The executive coach: Helper or healer? *Training Magazine*, 35: 30–36.
Flaherty J. (1999) *Coaching: Evoking Excellence in Others*. Burlington, MA: Elsevier Butterworth-Heinemann.
Flaherty J. (2005) *Coaching: Evoking Excellence In Others*, 2nd edn. Burlington, MA: Elsevier Butterworth-Heinemann.
Foucault, M. (1979) *Discipline and Punish: The Birth of the Prison*. London: Penguin
Foucault, M. (2006) *The History of Madness*. Oxford: Routledge.
Fredrickson, B.L., Mancuso, R.A., Branigan, C. and Tugade, M.M. (2000) The undoing effect of positive emotions, *Motivation and Emotion*, 24: 237–258.

Freedman, M. (1999) *The Kindness of Strangers: Adult Mentors, Urban Youth and the New Voluntarism*. Cambridge: Cambridge University Press.

Gallwey, T. (1974) *The Inner Game of Tennis*. London: Jonathan Cape.

Garmezy, N. (1982) Foreword. In E.E. Werner and R.S. Smith (eds), *Vulnerable But Invincible: A Study of Resilient Children*. New York: McGraw-Hill.

Garvey, B. (1995) Healthy signs for mentoring, *Education and Training*, 37(5): 12–19.

Garvey, B. (1998) Mentoring in the market place: studies of learning at work. Unpublished PhD thesis, University of Durham.

Garvey, B. (1999) Mentoring and the changing paradigm, *Mentoring and Tutoring*, 7(1): 41–54.

Garvey, B. (2005) A case of culture. In D. Megginson, D. Clutterbuck, B. Garvey, P. Stokes, and R. Garrett-Harris (eds), *Mentoring in Action*, 2nd edn. London: Kogan Page.

Garvey, B. (2006) Let me tell you a story, *International Journal of Mentoring and Coaching*, IV(1).

Garvey, B. and Alred, G. (2001) Mentoring and the tolerance of complexity, *Futures*, 33: 519–530.

Garvey, B. and Garrett-Harris, R. (2005) The benefits of mentoring: a literature review, *Report for East Mentors Forum*, Sheffield Hallam University: Mentoring and Coaching Research Unit.

Garvey, B. and Williamson, B. (2002) *Beyond Knowledge Management: Dialogue, Creativity and the Corporate Curriculum*. Harlow: Pearson Education.

Garvey, B., Alred, G. and Smith, R. (1996) First person mentoring, *Career Development International*: 10–14.

Garvey, B., Stokes, P. and Megginson, D. (2009) *Coaching and Mentoring Theory and Practice*. London: Sage.

Geertz, C. (ed.) (1971) Myth, *Symbol and Culture*. New York: Norton.

Gibb, S. and Hill, P. (2006) From trail-blazing individualism to a social construction community: modelling knowledge construction in coaching, *International Journal of Mentoring and Coaching*, 4(2).

Goldman, L. (1984) Warning: the Socratic Method can be dangerous, *Educational Leadership*, 42(1): 57–62.

Gorby, C. B. (1937) Everyone gets a share of the profits, *Factory Management & Maintenance*, 95: 82–83.

Gotham, H.J. (2004) Diffusion of mental health and substance abuse treatments: development, dissemination, and implementation, *Clinical Psychology: Science & Practice*, 11: 160–178.

Grant, A.M. (2003) The impact of life coaching on goal attainment, metacognition and mental health, *Social Behavior and Personality,* 31(3).

Grant, A.M. (2007) Past, present and future: the evolution of professional coaching and coaching psychology. In S. Palmer and A. Whybrow (eds), *Handbook of Coaching Psychology: A Guide for Practitioners*. Hove: Routledge.

Grant, A.M. and Cavanagh, M. (2004) Toward a profession of coaching: sixty-five years of progress and challenges for the future, *International Journal of Evidence Based Coaching and Mentoring,* 2(1): 1–16.

Grant, A. and O'Hara, B. (2006) The self-presentation of commercial Australian life coaching schools: cause for concern? *International Coaching Psychology Review,* 1(2): 20–32.

Grant, A.M. and Palmer, S. (2002) Coaching psychology workshop. In S. Palmer and A. Whybrow (2007) *Handbook of Coaching Psychology: A Guide to Practitioners*. London: Routledge.

Gray, D. (1988) Socratic seminars: basic education and reformation. In A. Rud Jnr. (ed.), The Use and Abuse of Socrates in Present Day Teaching, *Educational Policy Archives,* 5(20).

Groot, W. (1996) Het rendement van bedrijfsopleidingen. In J.W.M. Kessels (ed.) *Corporate Education: The Ambivalent Perspective of Knowledge Productivity*. Leiden University: Centre for Education and Instruction.

Grossman, J.B. and Tierney, J.P. (1998) Does mentoring work? An impact study of the Big Brothers Big Sisters Program, *Public/Private Ventures Evaluation Review,* 22(3): 403–426.

Grugulis, I. (1998) 'Real' managers don't do NVQs: a review of the new management 'standards', *Employee Relations,* 20: 383–403.

Grugulis, I. (2000) The Management NVQ: a critique of the myth of relevance, *Journal of Vocational Education and Training*, 52: 79–99.

Habermas, J. (1974) *Theory and Practice* (first published in 1971 as *Theorie und Praxis*). Portsmouth: Heinemann.

Harrison, R. and Smith, R. (2001) Practical judgement: its implications for knowledge development and strategic capability. In B. Hellgren, and J. Lowstedt (eds), *Management in the Thought-Full Enterprise, European Ideas on Organizing*. Fagbokforlaget, Poland: OZGraf SA.

Hart, V., Blattner, J. and Leipsic, S. (2007) Coaching versus therapy: a perspective. In R.R. Kilburg and R.C. Diedrich (eds), *The Wisdom of Coaching: Essential Papers in Consulting Psychology for a World of Change*, pp. 267–274. Washington, DC: APA.

Held, B.S. (2004) The negative side of positive psychology, *Journal of Humanistic Psychology,* 44(1): 9–41.

Honoria (1793) *The Female Mentor or Select Conversations,* Vols 1 and 2. London: T. Cadell.

Honoria (1796) *The Female Mentor or select conversations*, Vol. 3. London: T. Cadell.

Hughes, J. (2003) *A Reflection on the Art and Practice of Mentorship*. Institutional Investor plc.

Hunt, J.M. and Weintraub, J.R. (2002) *The Coaching Manager: Developing Top Talent in Business*. London: Sage.

Hurley, A.E. and Fagenson-Eland, E.A. (1996) Challenges in cross-gender mentoring relationships: psychological intimacy, myths, rumours, innuendoes and sexual harassment, *Leadership & Organization Development Journal*, 17(3): 42–49.

Hutton, W. (1997) *The State to Come*. London: Vintage.

Jarvis, P. (1992) *Paradoxes of Learning: On Becoming an Individual in Society*. San Francisco, CA: Jossey-Bass Higher Education Series.

Johnson, P. and Duberley, J. (2000) *Understanding Management Research*. London: Sage.

Johnson, S.K., Geroy, G.D. and Orlando, V.G. (1999) The mentoring model theory: dimensions in mentoring protocols, *Career Development International*, 4(7): 384–391.

Jung, C.J. (1958) *Psyche and Symbol*. New York: Doubleday.

Kampa-Kokesch, S. and Anderson, M. (2001) Executive coaching: a comprehensive review of the literature, *Consulting Psychology Journal: Practice and Research*, 53(4).

Kay, L.H. and Young, J.L. (1986) Socratic Teaching in Social Studies, *Social Studies*, 77(4): 158–61.

Kessels, J. (1996) *The Corporate Curriculum*. Inaugural Lecture, The University of Leiden, NL.

Kierkegaard, S. (1998) In E.H.V. Hong and E.H. Hong *Kierkegaard's Writings, XXII: The Point of View*. pp. 45. New Jersey: Princeton University Press.

Kilburg, R.R. (2004). Trudging toward Dodoville: conceptual approaches and case studies in executive coaching, *Consulting Psychology Journal: Practice and Research*, 56: 203–213.

Kimball, B.A. (1986) *Orators and Philosophers: A History of the Idea of Liberal Education*, New York: Teachers College Press.

Kirchmeyer, C. (2005) The effects of mentoring on academic careers over time: testing performance and political perspectives, *Human Relations*, 58(5): 637–660.

Kolb, D.A. (1984) *Experiential Learning*. Englewood Cliffs, NJ: Prentice Hall.

Kram, K.E (1983) Phases of the mentor relationship, *Academy of Management Journal*, 26(4): 608–625.

Kram, K.E. (1985) *Mentoring at Work: Developmental Relationships in Organizational Life*. Glenview, IL: Scott, Foresman.

Kram, K.E. and Chandler, D.E. (2005) Applying an adult development perspective to developmental networks, *Career Development International*, 10(6/7): 548–566.

Krohn, D. (2004) Four indispensable features of Socratic dialogue. In R. Saran and B. Neisser (eds), *Enquiring Minds: Socratic Dialogue in Education*. Stoke on Trent: Trentham Books.

Lankau, M. and Scandura, T. (2002) An investigation of personal learning in mentoring relationships: content, antecedents and consequences, *Academy of Management Journal*, 45(4): 779–790.

Law, H., Ireland, S. and Hussain, Z. (2007) *The Psychology of Coaching, Mentoring and Learning*. Chichester: Wiley.

Layder, D. (1994) *Understanding Social Theory*. London: Sage.

Lee, G. (2003) *Leadership Coaching: From Personal Insight to Organisational Performance*. London: CIPD.

Lester, S. (1994) Management standards: a critical approach, *Competency*, 2(1): 28–31.

Levin-Epstein, M. (2003) Use mentoring to promote teamwork, improve productivity, *Staff Leader*, 16(5): 1–3.

Levinson, D.J., Darrow, C.N., Klein, E.B., Levinson, M.H. and McKee, B. (1978) *The Seasons of a Man's Life*. New York: Knopf.

Lewin, K. (1951) *Field Theory in Social Sciences*. New York: Harper Row.

Linley, A.P. and Harrington, S. (2005) Psychology: perspectives on integration, *The Coaching Psychologist*, 1 July 13. The British Psychological Society.

Linley, A.P., Joseph, S. and Boniwell, I. (eds) (2003) In a positive light [Special Issue], *The Psychologist*, 16(3).

Loan-Clarke, J. (1996) The Management Charter Initiative: a critique of management standards/NVQs, *Journal of Management Development*, 15: 4–17.

Lowman R.L. (2005) Executive coaching: the road to Dodoville needs paving with more than good assumptions, *Consulting Psychology Journal: Practice and Research*, 57: 90–96.

Lyotard, J-F. (2005) The postmodern condition: a report on knowledge (Manchester, Manchester University Press). In M. Pedler, J. Burgoyne and C. Brook (eds), What has action learning learned to become? *Action Learning: Research and Practice*, 2(1): 49–68.

McAuley, M.J. (2003) Transference, countertransference and mentoring: the ghost in the process, *British Journal of Guidance & Counselling*, 31(1): 11–23.

McAuley, J., Duberley, J. and Johnson, P. (2007) *Organizational Theory: Challenges and Perspectives*. Harlow: Pearson Education.

McClelland, D. and Burnham, D. (1976) Power is the great motivator. In V.H. Vroom and E.L. Deci (eds), *Management and Motivation*. Harmondsworth: Penguin.

McDermott, I. and Jago, W. (2005) *The Coaching Bible: The Essential Handbook*. London: Piatkus.

Megginson, D. (2000) Current issues in mentoring, *Career Development International*, 5/4/5: 256–260.

Megginson, D. (2007) Is goal setting really essential for coaching success? *People Management*, October.

Megginson, D. and Boydell, T. (1979) *A Manager's Guide to Coaching*. London: Chartered Institute of Personnel and Development.

Megginson, D. and Clutterbuck, D. (1995) *Mentoring in Action*. London: Kogan Page.

Megginson, D., Clutterbuck, D., Garvey, B., Stokes, P. and Garrett-Harris, R. (eds) (2005) *Mentoring in Action*, 2nd edn. London: Kogan Page.

Moberg, D.J., Velasquez, M. (2004) The ethics of mentoring, *Business Ethics Quarterly*, 14(1): 95–102.

Morgan, L.M. and Davidson, M.J. (2008) Sexual dynamics in mentoring relationships – a critical review, *British Journal of Management*, 19(1): S120–S129.

Morris, B. and Tarpley, N.A. (2000) So you're a player, do you need a coach?, *Fortune*, 141(4).

Mullen, E. (1994) Framing the mentoring relationship as an information exchange, *Human Resource Management Review*, 4: 257–281.

Murray, M. and Owen, M.A. (1991) *Beyond the Myths and Magic of Mentoring*. San Francisco, CA: Jossey-Bass.

Neenan, M. (2009) Using Socratic questioning in coaching, *Journal of Rational-Emotive and Cognitive-Behavior Therapy*, 27(4): 249–264.

Nielsen, A. E. and Nørreklit, H. (2009) A discourse analysis of the disciplinary power of management coaching, *Denmark Society and Business Review*, 4(3): 202–214.

Nietzsche, F. (1974) *The Gay Science*. London: Vintage Books.

Noe, R.A. (1988) Women and mentoring: a review and research agenda, *Academy of Management Review*, 13(1): 65–79.

Nonaka, I. (1991) The knowledge creating company, *Harvard Business Review*, Nov–Dec: 96–104.

Parker, D. and Stacey, R.D. (1994) *Chaos Management and Economics*. Hobart Paper 125. London: Institute of Economic Affairs.

Parsloe, E. and Wray, M. (2000) *Coaching and Mentoring: Practical Methods to Improve Learning*. London: Kogan Page.

Pedler, M., Burgoyne, J. and Brook, C. (2005) What has action learning learned to become? *Action Learning: Research and Practice*, 2(1): 49–68.

Piaget, J. (1970) *Genetic Epistemology*. New York: Columbia University Press.

Phillips, R. (1996) Coaching for higher performance, *Employee Counselling Today*, 8(4): 29–32.

Polanyi, M. (1958) *Personal Knowledge: Towards a Post-critical Philosophy*. London: Routledge and Kegan Paul.

Porter, T.M. (1995) *Trust in Numbers*. Princeton: Princeton University Press.

Prahald, C.K. and Bettis, R. (1996) The dominant logic: a new linkage between diversity and performance. In K. Starkey (ed.), *How Organisations Learn*. London: International Thompson Business Press.

Ragins, B.R. (1989) Barriers to mentoring: the female manager's dilemma, *Human Relations*, 42(1): 1–23.

Ragins, B.R. (1994) *Gender and Mentoring: A Research Agenda*. Presented at the 40th annual meeting of the South Eastern Psychological Association, New Orleans, LA, April.

Ragins, B.R. and Cotton, J.L. (1991) Easier said than done: gender differences in perceived barriers to gaining a mentor, *Academy of Management Journal*, 34(4): 939–952.

Ragins, B.R. and Cotton, J.L. (1996) Jumping the hurdles: barriers to mentoring for women in organizations, *Leadership & Organization Development Journal*, 17(3): 37–41.

Ragins, B.R. and Cotton, J.L. (1999) Mentor functions and outcomes: a comparison of men and women in formal and informal mentoring relationships, *Journal of Applied Psychology*, 84(4): 529–550.

Ragins, B.R. and Scandura, T.A. (1994) Gender differences in expected outcomes of mentoring relationships, *Academy of Management Journal*, 37: 957–971.

Ragins, B.R. and Scandura, T.A. (1999) Burden or blessing? Expected costs and benefits of being a mentor, *Journal of Organisational Behavior*, 20(4): 493–509.

Reed, M. and Harvey, D.L. (1992) The new science and the old: complexity and realism, *Social Sciences Journal of the Theory of Social Science Behaviour*, 22(4): 353–380.

Reich, M.H. (1986) The mentor connection, *Personnel*, 63(2): 265–276.

Rix, M. and Gold, J. (2000) With a little help from my academic friend: mentoring change agents, *Mentoring and Tutoring*, 8(1): 47–62.

Rogers, C. (1961) *A Therapist's View of Psychotherapy: On Becoming a Person*. London: Constable and Company.

Rogers, C. (1969) *Freedom to Learn*. Columbus, OH: Merrill.

Rosinski, P. (2004) *Coaching Across Cultures*. London: Nicholas Brealey.

Rud, A.G. Jr (1997) The use and abuse of socrates in present day teaching, *Educational Policy Analysis Archives*, 5(20): 1–14.

Rushdie, S. (1991) *1,000 Days 'Trapped Inside a Metaphor'*, Columbia University Speech on 12 December. Published in *The New York Times*.

Russell, B. (1928) *Sceptical Essays*. London: Allen and Unwin Ltd.

Schon, D.A. (1983) *The Reflective Practitioner*. New York: Basic Books.

Schulman, L.S. (1998) Conclusion. In G. Alred, B. Garvey and R.D. Smith (eds), Pas de deux – learning in conversations, *Career Development International*, 3(7): 308–314.

Sendak, M. (1963) *Where The Wild Things Are*. New York: Harper & Row.

Senge, P.M. (1992) *The Fifth Discipline*. Chatham: Century Business.

Sheehy, G. (1976) *Passages: Predictable Crises of Adult Life*. New York: Dotton.

Sheehy, G. (1996) *New Passages: Mapping Your Life Across Time*. London: Harper Collins.

Sherman, S. and Freas, A. (2004) The Wild West of executive coaching, *Harvard Business Review*, November: 82–84.

Skolimowski, H. (1992) *Living Philosophy: Ecophilosophy as a Tree of Life*. London: Arkana.

Smith, B. (1990) Mutual mentoring on projects, *Journal of Management Development*, 90: 51–57.

Soros, G. (2000) *Open Society: Reforming Global Capitalism*. London: Little, Brown and Co.

Stacey, R.D. (1995) The science of complexity: an alternative perspective for strategic change processes, *Strategic Management Journal*, 16: 477–495.

Starkey, K. (1998) What can we learn from the learning organisation? *Human Relations*, 51: 531–546.

Starr, J. (2002) *The Coaching Manual, The Definitive Guide*. Harlow: Pearson Education.

Starr, J. (2008) *The Coaching Manual, The Definitive Guide*, 2nd edn. Harlow: Pearson Education.

Stelter, R. (2009) Coaching as a reflective space in a society of growing diversity – towards a narrative, postmodern paradigm, *International Coaching Psychology Review*, 4(2): 209–219.

Stober, D.R. (2006) Coaching from the humanistic perspective. In D.R. Stober and A.M. Grant (eds), *Evidence Based Coaching Handbook*. Englewood, NJ: Wiley.

Stokes, P. (2010) *What is truth?* pp. 3–4. Unpublished essay, Sheffield Hallam University (for access email: r.garvey@shu.ac.uk).

Stone, I.F. (1988) *The Trial of Socrates*. Boston, MA: Little, Brown.

Sullivan, R. (1995) Entrepreneurial learning and mentoring, *International Journal of Entrepreneurial Behaviour & Research,* 6(3): 160–175.

Swailes, S. and Roodhouse, S. (2003) Structural barriers to the take-up of Higher Level NVQs, *Journal of Vocational Education and Training,* 55(1): 85–110.

Turban, D. and Dougherty, T. (1994) Role of protégé personality in receipt of mentoring and career success, *Academy of Management Journal*, 37(3): 688–702.

UK Executive Coaching Report (2004) *Association for Coaching*, December.

Von Krogh, G., Roos, J. and Slocum, K. (1994) An essay on corporate epistemology, *Strategic Management Journal*, 15: 53–71.

Vygotsky, L.S. (1978) *Mind in Society: The Development of Higher Psychological Processes*. Cambridge, MA: Harvard University Press.

Vygotsky, L.S. (1981) The genesis of higher mental functions. In J. Wertsch (ed.), *The Concept of Activity in Soviet Psychology*. New York: Armonk.

Vygotsky, L.S. (1985a) In J. V. Wertsch (ed.), *Vygotsky and the Social Formation of Mind*. Cambridge, MA: Harvard University Press.

Vygotsky, L.S. (1985b) In J.V. Wertsch (ed.), *Culture, Communication and Cognition: Vygotskian Perspectives*. Cambridge: Cambridge University Press.

Wampold, B.E., Mondin, G.W., Moody, M., Stich, F., Benson, K. and Ahn, H. (1997) A meta-analysis of outcome studies comparing bona-fide psychotherapies: empirically, "all must have prizes", *Psychological Bulletin,* 122: 203–215.

Webster, F. (1980) *The New Photography: Responsibility in Visual Communication*. London: John Calder.

Weick, K. (1995) *Sensemaking in Organizations (Foundations for Organizational Science)*. Thousand Oaks, CA: Sage.

Whitmore, J. (1997) *Need, Greed and Freedom*. Shaftesbury: Element Books.

Whitmore, J. (2002) *Coaching for Performance: GROWing people, performance and purpose,* 3rd edn. London: Nicholas Brealey.

Whitmore, J. (2003) Coaching: Les techniques d'entraînement du sport de haut niveau au service de l'entreprise. In G. Arnaud (ed.), A coach or a couch? A Lacanian perspective on executive coaching and consulting, *Human Relations,* 56(9): 1131–1154.

Whitmore, J. (2004) Coaching for performance. In P. Ferrar (ed.), Defying definition: competences in coaching and mentoring, *International Journal of Evidence Based Coaching and Mentoring*, 2(2).

Williams, D.I. and Irving, J.A. (2001) Coaching: An unregulated, unstructured and (potentially) unethical process, *The Occupational Psychologist*, 42: 3–7.

Willis, P. (2005) European Mentoring and Coaching Council, *Competency Research Project: Phase 2*, June. Watford: EMCC.

Wilson, C. (2007) *Best Practice in Performance Coaching: A Handbook for Leaders, Coaches, HR Professionals and Organizations*. London: Kogan Page.

Wilson, J.A. and Elman, N.S. (1990) Organizational benefits of mentoring, *Academy of Management Executive*, 4: 88–94.

Winstanley, D. and Stuart-Smith, K. (1996) Policing performance: the ethics of performance management, *Personnel Review*, 25(6): 66–84.

Wood, A.W. (1970) *Kant's Moral Religion*. Ithaca, NY: Cornell University Press.

Zaleznik, A. (1997) Managers and leaders: are they different? *Harvard Business Review*, May–June: 67–78.

Zeus, P. and Skiffington, S. (2000) *The Complete Guide to Coaching at Work*. Sydney: McGraw-Hill.

Zey, M.C. (1984) *The Mentor Connection: Strategic Alliances in Corporate Life*. Homewood, IL: Dow Jones-Irving.

web references

Active Community Unit, Home Office, UK (2011) http://www.mandbf.org.uk/about/definitions/, accessed 23 March 2011.

Bresser, F. (2009) *Global Coaching Survey*, Frank Bresser Consulting, www.frank-bresser-consulting.com. accessed 26 May 2011.

Bresser, F. (2008) *European Coaching Survey*, Bresser Consulting, www.bresser-consulting.com. accessed 26 May 2011.

Brock, V.G. (2008) *Grounded Theory of The Roots and Emergence of Coaching*. An unpublished Dissertation Submitted in Partial Fulfilment of the Requirements for the Degree Doctor of Philosophy in Coaching and Human Development International University of Professional Studies Maui, 2008 http://www.nobco.nl/files/onderzoeken/Brock_Vikki_dissertatie__2_.pdf. accessed 26 May 2011.

Grant, A. M. (2001) *Towards a Psychology of Coaching*, Coaching Psychology Unit, School of Psychology, University of Sydney, Australia,http://74.125.155.132/scholar?q=cache:KwNWl5hkRCQJ:

scholar.google.com/+Grant+coaching+psychology&hl=en&as_sdt=2000 accessed 26 May 2011.

Kanai, T., Fujii, H. and Hirakimoto, H. (1996) *The impacts of Mentorship upon Middle Managers' Psychological Empowerment and their Leadership Behaviour: Empirical Analyses of Direct and Indirect Impacts,* Paper presented at Mitsubishi Bank Foundation/IBM Conference on New Imperatives in Managing Revolutionary Change in Ito, Japan, August http://www.lib.kobe-u.ac.jp/repository/81000823.pdf, accessed 23 July 2010.

Marx, K. (1852) The Eighteenth Brumaire of Louis Bonaparte, http://www.marxists.org/archive/marx/works/1852/18th-brumaire/, accessed 23 July 2010.

Megginson, D. (2007) Is goal setting really essential for coaching success? October http://www.peoplemanagement.co.uk/pm/articles/2007/10/isgoalsettingreallyessentialforcoachingsuccess.htm, accessed 6 August 2010.

Mooney, P. (2008) *The Dublin Declaration on Coaching,* Version 1.3, Global Community of Coaches, Dublin http://www.pdf.net/Files/Dublin%20Declaration%20on%20Coaching.pdf, accessed 23 July 2010.

Murray, J. (2010) Smile or Die: How Positive Thinking Fooled America and the World by Barbara Ehrenreich, *The Observer*, 10 January 2010, http://www.guardian.co.uk/books/2010/jan/10/smile-or-die-barbara-ehrenreich, accessed 25 March 2011.

Nietzsche, F. (1873, Revised Edition, 2010) On the Use and Abuse of History for Life, Translated by Ian Johnston, Vancouver Island University, Nanaimo, BC, Canada. http://records.viu.ca/~johnstoi/Nietzsche/history.htm, accessed 26 April 2010.

http://unjobs.org/vacancies/1279743103672, accessed 6 August 2010.

Russell, B. (1928) 'Sceptical Essays' London: George Allen & Unwin Ltd. http://www.brainyquote.com/quotes/b/bertrandru408841.html, accessed 22 March 2011.

Index